Gender Inequalities in
Nursing Careers

Gender Inequalities in Nursing Careers

LOUISE R. FINLAYSON

AND

JAMES Y. NAZROO

POLICY STUDIES INSTITUTE
LONDON

UNIVERSITY OF WESTMINSTER

PSI is a wholly owned subsidiary of the University of Westminster

© **Policy Studies Institute, 1997**

A CIP catalogue record of this book is available from the British Library.

ISBN 0 85374 737 7
PSI report number 854

Typesetting by PCS Mapping & DTP, Newcastle upon Tyne
Printed in Great Britain by Page Bros, Norwich

Policy Studies Institute is one of Europe's leading research organisations undertaking studies of economic, industrial and social policy and the workings of political institutions. The Institute is a registered charity and is not associated with any political party, pressure group or commercial interest.

For further information contact
Policy Studies Institue, 100 Park Village East, London NW1 3SR
Tel: 0171 468 0468   Fax: 0171 388 0914   Email: pubs@psi.org.uk

The NHS must set the pace in the 1990s as the best employer of women. This is not 'positive discrimination' but 'enlightened self interest' ... it needs to recruit, retrain and provide the best career opportunities for women at all levels in the NHS. It must not be 'as good as' but better than other employers at providing imaginative and flexible arrangements to enable women to combine work and family responsibilities.

Virginia Bottomley,
then Secretary of State for Health,
May 1991
(cited in NUPE 1992:3)

Contents

List of Illustrations

TABLES

Boxes

Figures

Foreword

I would like to commend to you this valuable work by the Policy Studies Institute. A thorough going piece of research, it provides confirmation and a sound factual basis for something that has long been felt to be the case: that many female nurses do not progress in their careers as quickly, or as far, as their male colleagues.

Ninety per cent of our nurses are female, the overwhelming majority of the workforce. Half of them have a child under the age of sixteen. It is this dependent child who is shown to be the most significant indicator of labour market participation by the mother. The non-availability of flexible working patterns and childcare facilities are seen as major obstacles both to employment and career progress. These obstacles are present even at the most junior levels, calling into question the concept of a glass ceiling in nursing, but there is particular lack of part-time and flexible opportunities in management and in senior nursing posts.

Our nurses are in the frontline of patient care in the NHS. We need to show that they are valued, that the service needs their skills and that it will support them in balancing the demands of their careers with family responsibilities. An equal opportunities policy which states that all posts are open to women, but does nothing to address historic organisational norms, is a hollow boast.

If the NHS is to continue to attract and retain nurses, this timely research has lessons for us all.

Yvonne Moores
Chief Nursing Officer
Department of Health (England)
April 1998

Acknowledgements

The survey on which this volume is based was carried out by the Policy Studies Institute and funded by the Department of Health. We are grateful to the Department of Health and our colleagues at the Policy Studies Institute who worked on the original study - Sharon Beishon, Satnam Virdee and Ann Hagell - for making the data available to us.

The work carried out for this volume was also sponsored by the Department of Health. During its preparation, we were fortunate to have had support and advice from a number of friends and colleagues in the Policy Studies Institute, in universities and the NHS. We are particularly grateful to Mary Ann Elston, Ann Hagell, Karen Iley, Hilary Metcalf, Satnam Virdee and two anonymous referees, all of who made contributions that led to significant improvements to the volume. Other colleagues at the Policy Studies Institute also made significant contributions to this volume, in particular Jo O'Driscoll (publications) and Neil Churchill (external relations). We would also like to thank Susan Lonsdale (Department of Health) and Pam Harris (NHS Executive, Equal Opportunities Unit) for their support.

Above all, we are grateful to the 14,300 nurses who took the time to participate in the survey used in this study. Responsibility for this volume and its conclusions lies with the authors.

Louise Finlayson
James Nazroo
April 1998

CHAPTER 1

Introduction and Methodology

BACKGROUND

There is a large body of research evidence which suggests that men have greater career success in the nursing profession than women (Davies and Roser, 1986; Waite *et al.*, 1990; IHMS, 1995). This report sets out to examine the full extent of men's career advantage in nursing and explores the importance of various factors in explaining the influence of gender on the career paths of nurses. The report is based on the largest ever survey of nurses employed by the NHS in England and Wales, carried out in 1994. The survey is representative of both qualified and unqualified nursing staff and junior and senior nurses. Before describing the survey and the approach taken for the analysis in more detail, we first outline ways of understanding gender differences in paid work and describe existing research on gender differences in the labour market in general then, more specifically, in the nursing profession.

THEORETICAL PERSPECTIVES ON WOMEN IN EMPLOYMENT

Article 119 of the Treaty of Rome (1957) states that 'each Member State shall ... ensure and subsequently maintain the application of the principle that men and women should receive equal pay for equal work'. However, it was not until the late 1960s and early 1970s that the interests of women in employment began to be represented. The Defrenne cases[1] in the European Court of Justice laid the foundation for a large body of case law and provided the impetus for legislation on equal pay and equal treatment relating to employment and to social security matters. It has been nearly three decades since The Equal Pay Act (1970) and The Sex Discrimination Act (1975) became effective in Britain. But women's inequality in the labour market remains an important issue of concern (Humphries and Rubery, 1995). As will be

---

1. Gabrielle Defrenne was the first women to refer a series of actions alleging gender discrimination in terms of pay, conditions and pensions to the European Court of Justice (Prechal and Burrows, 1990).

discussed below, this inequality of opportunity is constrained by social and organisational barriers, and by women's own internalised standards and choices about the appropriate mix between paid and home work.

There is now a voluminous economic and sociological literature devoted to women and paid work. The investigation of economic equality in the labour market has sought to estimate the extent of sex discrimination. Labour market discrimination has been defined as being present when women with abilities, education, training and experience that are similar to those of men have poorer access to paid work and promotion, and have lower wages (Berndt, 1991). However, the focus of many economic studies has been on only one of these factors, wage differentials, where it has been shown that women earn 80 per cent of men's weekly earnings in the public sector and just 67 per cent in the private sector (*Financial Times*, 28th January 1997). But, it is important to recognise that the presence of such a wage gap, or other forms of occupational disadvantage, is not in itself evidence of discrimination. As the definition derived from Berndt (1991) suggests, it will in part be comprised of gender differences in what economists term 'human capital attributes'.[2]

Thus, the major empirical work lies within the Human Capital Framework pioneered by Becker (1957; 1964; 1985) and refined by Mincer and Polachek (1974). The focus of many studies to date has been the measurement of discrimination after taking into account gender variations in work experience, education, training and other relevant factors. In empirical work in this tradition, the gap that exists between male and female wages after taking into account such gender differences in human capital is attributed to discrimination (in the absence of other explanations). Collectively, such empirical estimates have established that gender discrimination is a feature of the British labour market, but the estimated extent of such discrimination varies between studies (Wright and Ermisch, 1991; Paci, Joshi and Makepeace, 1995).

Another prominent feature of the British labour market is the extent of occupational segregation by gender (Millward and Woodland, 1995). A review of the substantial literature on this can be found in Sloane *et al.* (1993). It is suggested that there are two types of occupational segregation: vertical and horizontal. Vertical segregation occurs when men and women in the same occupation attain different hierarchical levels, that is, where men are found in higher grades than women, who are, in turn, concentrated in the lower grades (Callender,

---

2. The concept of human capital is based on 'the idea that education and training constitute an investment in individuals, which is analogous to investment in machinery.' (Elliot, 1991: 154)

1996). Within the National Health Service (NHS), for example, only 28 per cent of chief executive or general manager posts are held by women, and the figure is much lower in the private sector (Labour Research, 1997). Vertical segregation is commonly seen as a consequence of the 'glass ceiling' effect:

> *'Women are confronted by a glass ceiling when it comes to entering positions of power ... a ceiling that often requires a sledge-hammer to shatter! This glass ceiling is invisible but women experience it as a very real barrier when they vie for promotion to top jobs'.*
>
> (Davidson and Cooper, 1992: 15)

Horizontal segregation is the disproportionate representation of women in certain occupations. This can be demonstrated by the fact that a half of all women in employment, compared with less than a fifth of men (18 per cent), are found in just three types of occupation: clerical and secretarial; personal and protective services; and sales (Sly *et al.*, 1997). Initially, theories relating to this type of segmentation in the labour market adopted a dualistic approach, separating the labour market into 'primary' and 'secondary' sectors. The secondary sector consisted of low-status, low-paid jobs with little possibility of advancement and in which women are concentrated (Wilkinson, 1981). This theory has since been adapted into a more complex model describing a spectrum of labour market sectors, with women and men often competing in different sectors (Millward and Woodland, 1995). Millward and Woodland (1995) found evidence of substantial gender segregation between establishments, which had an adverse effect on the relative pay of women.

Nursing provides a good example of both types of occupational segregation. Women's numerical dominance within nursing and men's concentration within particular specialities in nursing (which is discussed later) are clear examples of horizontal occupational segregation. At the same time the well documented concentration of male nurses in more senior positions provides a clear example of vertical occupational segregation and how this occurs even in a female dominated occupation.

There are, of course, many determining factors for occupational status and earnings, which, consequently, can be seen as:

> *'a result of the interaction of a complex set of institutions, be they familial, legal or cultural, all of which serve to reinforce the existing sex inequality in home, work places and society.'*
>
> (Joseph, 1983: 205)

Therefore, women's economic disadvantage must be analysed within the broader cultural, social and political frameworks within which public policy is formed. The role of women in the family and at work, and attitudes towards work and home life are changing, but progress is uneven.

Despite the growing evidence of the extent and nature of the disadvantages faced by women in paid employment, the sociological debate on the reasons for this continues. On the one hand, researchers have argued that women's disadvantaged status in the labour market is a result of two main barriers: a social barrier resulting from a gender-based stereotyping of roles, leading to a conflict between domestic and paid work roles for women; and an organisational barrier encountered as a result of employers' policies and practices. Adherents to this view see little room for improvement in the position of women in the labour market until the traditional roles women play in society are fundamentally altered and organisational 'norms' significantly modified to include greater flexibility in employment strategies. In the meantime, it is contended that the 'majority of women are trapped in the vicious circle of low pay, inability to afford full-day childcare and part-time employment' (Ginn *et al.*, 1996: 169).

On the other hand, it has been argued that women's orientation to work differs from that of men. Hakim (1995), for example, argues that 'sex differentials in employment experience are due to *personal choice* as much as to sex discrimination'. According to this perspective, traditional gender role attitudes condition employment decisions, with women polarised into two groups – 'career-centred' and 'home-centred' – though this is, perhaps, partly a reflection of class differences. Research has shown that many female managers, for example, have chosen the former role and have 'clearly decided that childlessness is a precondition for a successful managerial career' (Wajcman, 1996: 620). Of course, it is possible that such differences in career orientation are a consequence of stereotyping and/or differential success or opportunities in the labour market rather than personal choice – if women experience less success, or believe that they are likely to have less success, they may be more likely to focus on their roles at home.

These theoretical approaches set the context within which we can now examine the position of women in the labour market in general and, more specifically, in the nursing profession.

WOMEN'S POSITION IN THE LABOUR MARKET[3]

One of the most significant changes in the British labour market since the 1950s has been the rise in the female labour-force. Currently, 71 per cent of women of working age (16–59) are economically active, compared with 64 per cent in 1981 and just 43 per cent in 1951 (Sly *et al.*, 1997; Hakim, 1993). The expansion of women's employment has been attributed to the increase of part-time employment and the growth in labour-force participation of women with young children.

Despite the rise in the proportion of working mothers, the most significant predictor of women's labour-market participation remains whether or not she has a dependent child. In particular, the age of her youngest child has a strong influence on paid employment, with pre-school children being particularly important. Table 1.1 shows employment rates for women by the age of their youngest child. Overall, 67 per cent of all women of working age are in paid employment, but this ranges from 48 per cent for women whose youngest child is under 5 to three-quarters of women whose youngest is aged 11–15. This compares with 77 per cent for all men of working age (16–64).

As well as the age of her youngest child, a woman's economic activity is positively associated with her educational level. For example, among women with pre-school children, 74 per cent of women with A-levels or higher are economically active compared with 31 per cent of women with no educational qualifications.

Although the overall labour-market participation rates for men and women have been converging in recent years, significant differences in their employment patterns remain. Notably, there is a higher incidence of part-time work among women and a greater proportion of women

Table 1.1 Employment rates by age of youngest child

	Per cent employed
Women aged 16–59	
With children aged 0–4 years	48
With children aged 5–10 years	65
With children aged 11–15 years	75
With no dependent children	71
All	*67*
Men aged 16–64	77

Source: Labour Force Survey, Spring 1996 (Sly *et al.*, 1997)

3. The following data are taken from Sly et al., 1997 and are based on the Labour Force Survey, Spring 1996.

than men take career breaks, most commonly to raise a family. Overall, more than four-fifths of those working part-time are women. Once again this is related to having dependent children – nearly two-thirds (63 per cent) of employed women with dependent children work part-time, compared with one-third of women with no dependent children and just 8 per cent of men.

Earlier we described how men and women are also found in different occupational sectors within the labour-market. For example, women form the majority in clerical and secretarial work (75 per cent), personal and protective services (65 per cent) and sales (64 per cent). In addition, although 70 per cent of women work in non-manual occupations compared with around half of men, women make up less than a third of those in managerial/administrative positions.

WOMEN IN THE NURSING PROFESSION

Career structures and pathways in nursing are both complex and have frequently changed.[4] Entry into nursing can occur through a number of routes, there are numerous post-basic qualifications that can be taken, numerous areas that can be specialised in, and the career movement of individuals can be downward and sideways as well as upward (Waite *et al.*, 1990; Davies with Conn, 1993). Upward movement can be into either management or education and generally leads out of the clinical area.

Patterns of career development for nurses are undoubtedly a reflection of nursing's relatively young and female work-force. For example, in 1992, 90 per cent of nurses were female and 40 per cent were younger than 35 (Department of Health, 1995), and according to the Policy Studies Institute's (PSI) 1994 survey, about three-quarters of nurses were cohabiting or married and about half had children under the age of 16 (Beishon *et al.*, 1995).

It is in this context that the greater success of male nurses compared to their female counterparts in achieving promotion has been an issue of concern. Men are not only overrepresented in senior posts – for example, in 1987 they made up 50 per cent of chief nurses/advisors and 57 per cent of directors of nurse education (Gaze, 1987) – they also achieve promotion more quickly than women (Davies and Rosser, 1986; Waite *et al.*, 1990; IHMS, 1995). Interestingly, those women who make it into senior management are more likely than men to be single and less likely to have children (Hutt, 1985; IHMS, 1995). In addition, men are located within particular specialities in nursing – for example, in 1992 almost 40 per cent of male nurses worked in mental health compared with just over 10 per cent of female nurses (Department of Health,

---

4. Nursing career structures are summarised in Box 1.1 later in this chapter.

1995). In terms of recruitment and retention in nursing, concern has also been repeatedly expressed about the large number of nurses who take career breaks and then do not return to nursing (Goss and Brown, 1991). Indeed, one of the goals contained in the Opportunity 2000 initiative 'Women in the NHS' was concerned with recruitment and retention, while another was concerned with downward mobility following career breaks.

These differences between the position of women and men in nursing need to be seen in the context of the position of women in the labour-market more generally. As previously discussed, issues of importance include career breaks in order to have children, part-time work and occupational segregation. Indeed, the presence of both horizontal and vertical segregation in nursing provides a unique opportunity to examine the extent and causes of gender-based inequalities in the labour market.

Previous studies have suggested that a number of factors are responsible for the greater success of men compared with women in nursing. They use similar frameworks to those that are used to explain the wider occupational disadvantages faced by women. For example, many focus on gender differences in roles and the greater compatibility of male family roles with traditional career structures (Mackay, 1989). At least part of the reason for women's slower progress in nursing is seen as a result of the need for career breaks and part-time work, and a lack of geographical mobility, in order to have and care for a family (Goss and Brown, 1991). This has led to recommendations aimed at making nursing (and other NHS) careers more adaptable to the needs of women, with a focus on the need for flexible working, job-sharing, career breaks and childcare (Caines and Hammond, 1996). Related to this set of explanations is the possibility that women may also be generally less orientated to career success. While there is some evidence to support this (Rogers, 1983; Skevington & Dawkes, 1988; Buchan *et al.*, 1989), the different orientations of men and women could, of course, be a result of their evaluation of both the likelihood and the costs of success, and the level of encouragement they receive from mentors (Hardy, 1986a). There is also contrary evidence that suggests that women are just as likely as men to be committed to nursing work and professional development (Davies and Rosser, 1986).

PREVIOUS SURVEYS OF WOMEN IN NURSING

The Royal College of Nursing has conducted a number of surveys on a 1 per cent sample of its membership (approximately 3,000 people). These have primarily focused on demographic profiles and attitudes.

In terms of gender differences in nursing they have shown that:

- Women are more likely than men to have taken career breaks (Buchan *et al.*, 1989).
- Younger nurses anticipate taking career breaks in the future and, while 99 per cent expect to return, over half of these expect to return to work part-time (Buchan and Seccombe, 1991).
- Taking career breaks in order to have children sometimes results in returning to part-time posts that are junior to the post that had been left (Waite *et al.*, 1989).
- Those with dependent children have slower career progression (over half have some sort of caring responsibility for children) (Seccombe and Ball, 1992).
- Having some flexibility in work hours and adequate crèche provision is important to women with dependent children (Buchan and Seccombe, 1991).
- Marital commitments may restrict women's career mobility (Buchan *et al.*, 1989).
- More men than women have post-basic qualifications (Buchan and Seccombe, 1991).
- Men are more likely than women to expect promotion (Waite and Hutt, 1987).

Other large-scale surveys have suggested that female nurses are less interested than males in promotion or the prospect of working in management (Rogers, 1983; Price Waterhouse, 1988).

There have also been smaller surveys on the career paths of senior nurses that have explored gender differences. These have shown that men take a shorter time to reach senior positions; that men in such positions were more likely than equivalent women to be both married and to have children at home; and that women who had always worked full-time had progressed more rapidly than those who had at some stage worked part-time (Davies and Rosser, 1984; Hardy, 1986a,b). These findings have been confirmed by a recent IHMS survey of senior nurses. This showed that: female senior nurses had taken almost twice as long as men to reach nursing officer level; that 40 per cent of women compared to 6 per cent of men had worked part-time at some stage in their careers; that women were almost four times more likely to have taken a career break, were likely to have taken their career breaks to have children, and were far more likely than men to return to a job of the same or lower status after their career break; and that job changes for men were more likely than for women to have resulted in home moves, changes in children's schools, and weekly commuting or living away from a partner or family for more than a month (IHMS, 1995).

Altogether this suggests that men have been more likely to follow traditional career patterns, they have been more successful in nursing careers, and that the NHS has not been sufficiently flexible in meeting the career needs of its female nurses. Some smaller regional studies of qualified nurses, who were not necessarily in senior positions, have also been undertaken. These have generally confirmed the importance of family commitments in hampering career progression and the failure of employers to take these into account, or to understand the difficulties faced by women working in the NHS (see, for example, Mackay, 1989).

None of this work, however, has been able to systematically address these issues in a large sample that is representative of both qualified and unqualified staff and covers the career paths of both junior and senior staff. Here we are fortunate in having access to a unique study, the largest ever survey of nurses containing a nationally representative sample of over 14,000 nursing, midwifery and auxiliary staff within the NHS, which includes more than 1,000 men.

METHODOLOGY AND AIMS

In 1994 the Department of Health commissioned the Policy Studies Institute to carry out a large postal survey of nurses[5] employed by the NHS in England and Wales, the findings from which were published as *Nursing in a Multi-Ethnic NHS* (Beishon *et al.*, 1995). The present study is based on a secondary analysis of that survey, which provides a unique opportunity to assess the extent of differences in the career progression of male and female nurses and the importance of various factors in explaining uncovered differences.

Sampling for the survey was carried out to enable an exploration of issues to do with ethnicity, which was the purpose of the initial study, and full details of the sampling process used can be found in Beishon *et al.* (1995). Key points were that sampling was carried out using lists of employees drawn from different types of NHS employer (such as District Health Authority, Trusts and Family Health Service Authorities) and that employers in areas with high and medium concentrations of ethnic minority populations were oversampled in order to ensure that the ethnic minority sample was large enough to address the aims of the initial study. However, the sampling strategy adopted allows the sample to be reweighted in order to make it representative of the NHS workforce in 1994, and all of the findings reported here have been subjected to this weighting procedure.

---

5. The study covered nursing and allied activities, including auxiliaries, midwives and health visitors. In general, the terms 'nurse', 'nursing' and 'nursing staff' are used in their broad meaning, unless otherwise stated.

Overall 91 employers were used to identify respondents to whom the postal questionnaire was sent. The achieved sample size is large enough to explore all of the relevant issues for this study: 14,330 nurses were included, reflecting a response rate of 62 per cent to the postal questionnaire used. This is the largest ever survey of nurses in England and Wales, and importantly it includes over 1000 men – a sample size that none of the previous surveys that have explored the issue of gender have been able to attain. The material covered was explicitly designed to allow career progression to be addressed. Information was collected on: demographic factors, such as age, marital status and having children under 16; educational status, including post-basic nursing qualifications; the ease of access to study opportunities; the nature of the respondent's post, including speciality, grade and whether part-time; whether career breaks had been taken and what for; motives for entering nursing; levels and dimensions of job satisfaction; and expectations of career development over the next three years.[6]

This allows the following three main issues to be addressed:

1. The differences between the locations of men and women in nursing, taking into account: qualified versus unqualified staff; enrolled and registered qualifications; nursing grade; post-basic training and qualifications; full- and part-time work; speciality worked in; and types of shifts worked.
2. The differences between the attitudes and expectations of men and women in nursing: reasons for entering nursing; areas of dissatisfaction with their posts; expectations of ease of access to training opportunities; and expectations for career development.
3. The role of key factors in explaining the different success of men and women in nursing. Here the focus will be on how far gender predicts current nursing grade (as shown in Box 1.1, this is a direct indicator of career success in nursing) after controlling for: differences in human capital (such as qualifications); differences in career orientation; and the effect of organisational structures on career progression.

There is, however, one important limitation to this survey. As described, sampling was carried out using lists of NHS employees. This means that nurses who were no longer directly employed by the NHS were not covered. This includes three groups: those working in the private sector; those working exclusively through nursing agencies (bank nurses); and those who were no longer working as a nurse. The

---

6. Full details of the questionnaire used can be found in the Appendix.

Box 1.1 The Occupational Structure of Nursing

If differences between nurses working in particular specialities are ignored, there are essentially three types of nurse within the NHS: Registered Nurses; Enrolled Nurses; and Nursing Auxiliaries/Healthcare Assistants.

The first two of these, Registered and Enrolled Nurses, have undergone specific nurse training – a three year course for Registered Nurses and a two year course for Enrolled Nurses – and are governed by the United Kingdom Central Council for Nursing, Midwifery and Health Visiting (UKCC). They are described as 'qualified nurses' in the text of this report.

Nursing Auxiliaries/Healthcare Assistants may well have undergone some form of training, such as National Vocational Qualifications (NVQs), but they do not have a specific nursing qualification and are not governed by the UKCC. Hence, they are described as 'unqualified nurses' in the text of this report.

In 1988 nursing grades were introduced to reflect pay and seniority. These range from A to I. Generally, grades A and B cover Nursing Auxiliaries/Healthcare Assistants, grades C to E cover Enrolled Nurses, and grades D to I cover Registered Nurses. For Registered Nurses, grades D and E are effectively non-management posts (which might also be occupied by Enrolled Nurses), grades F and G are ward-based management posts, while grades H and I tend to be non-ward-based management posts.

The restriction of Enrolled Nurses to grades C to E effectively limits them to non-management posts. It is possible for Enrolled Nurses to become Registered Nurses, by undertaking additional training on a 'conversion course', after which their career options open up.

In 1989 the first Project 2000 training courses started. In recent years both Enrolled Nurse training and traditional Registered Nurse training have ceased, and Nursing Auxiliaries have been renamed Healthcare Assistants. So, although Enrolled Nurses still exist in the NHS, students are no longer recruited onto these courses.

Project 2000 training courses lead to the Registered Nurse qualification and a Diploma in Nursing. Project 2000 had only recently been introduced when the survey on which this study was based was undertaken, so there has been no attempt to distinguish Project 2000 nurses from other Registered Nurses in the following analyses.

The introduction of nursing grades and Project 2000 has transformed the career structure of nurses. As these changes occurred only a few years before the survey used for this study was conducted, their implications should be considered when interpreting the findings presented and discussed in the following chapters.

second and third of these groups are particularly important for an exploration of gender differences in career progression. One of the key differences between men and women may be that women are more likely than men to give up nursing completely, or to only do bank nursing, which would allow them to exercise greater choice over their work patterns and enable them to fit in more comfortably with their domestic responsibilities. If either of these were the case, our reliance on a sample that was currently employed in the NHS would lead to an underestimation of gender differences in career progression. In addition, the use of a sample of currently employed nurses means that we can only partially address issues to do with the retention of nursing staff. This important limitation will be returned to as we discuss the findings of this study.

The other issue that needs to considered when interpreting the findings of this study is that the fieldwork was undertaken during a period of change within the NHS. Firstly, following the introduction of Project 2000, changes were occurring in the career structures of nurses. These are outlined in Box 1.1, which describes the occupational structure of nursing. This structure is the backdrop to and guides the analyses presented in subsequent chapters, so should be closely referred to by those unfamiliar with nursing. Secondly, following the introduction of the internal market, great upheaval was occurring in the NHS more generally. The internal market separated the roles of purchasers of health care and providers of health care, with many providers becoming more independent in the form of hospital trusts and fund-holding GP practices. Of course, the providers of services were the employers of the staff surveyed in this study, and we are unable to estimate how such changes may have influenced the responses made to the questionnaire. However, it is likely that at least the more subjective questions, such as those on job satisfaction and expectations for the future, may have been influenced in some way.

OVERVIEW OF THE VOLUME

Chapter 2 provides a description of the differences in the locations of men and women in nursing. The initial focus of the chapter is on the types of basic nursing qualification held, nursing grades and the distribution of men and women across specialities. Chapter 2 also describes differences in patterns of work, looking at shift patterns and hours worked. It goes on to examine how factors relating to human capital might vary across men and women, looking at qualifications held, age and experience. The extent to which men and women felt that they had opportunities for training and career development is also described. Finally, the chapter examines the extent to which differences emerge between senior (grade H or I) and junior (grade D to G) registered nurses and whether gender differences in the location of nurses remain when only senior registered nurses are examined.

Chapter 3 focuses on the extent to which there might be gender differences in the attitudes and expectations of nurses. It begins with an examination of the reasons given for entering nursing. From these reasons, scales are developed to describe three key motivations that male and female nurses had for undertaking nursing: their degree of 'career orientation'; the extent to which nursing provided personal fulfilment; and the pay and conditions offered. Gender differences across these scales are described. Chapter 3 then provides a description of the aspects of nursing that provided satisfaction and dissatisfaction for nursing staff and the extent of any difference between men and women in this. Finally, it shows gender differences in nurses' expectations for their future.

Chapter 4 considers the extent to which family responsibilities might contribute to the gender differences described in earlier chapters. It begins by describing the proportion of nurses that had children and how this varied by marital status and age. It goes on to describe whether nurses had taken career breaks and their reasons for taking such breaks. It then explores how working patterns, such as the shifts and hours worked, were related to having children and marital status. Finally, Chapter 4 describes how respondents felt about the childcare facilities offered by their employers.

Chapter 5 uses multivariate analysis to uncover explanations for the gender differences in nursing grade shown in Chapter 2. It focuses on registered nurses and shows the impact of various explanatory factors on the chances of being in various grade positions. The explanatory factors used are: those relating to human capital (for example, qualifications and experience); career orientation; specialities worked in; and 'family friendly' working patterns (taking career breaks, working part-time and working particular shift patterns).

Finally, the conclusion provides a summary of the key findings of this study. It then considers how the findings might be interpreted and the extent to which the study has explained gender inequalities in nursing career progression. The implications of the findings for policy are then discussed.

CHAPTER 2

The Position of Men and Women in Nursing

INTRODUCTION

This chapter is concerned with providing a basic description of the job-related differences between male and female nurses. The initial focus is on differences in the distribution of men and women across different types of nursing qualification, nursing grades, and specialities worked in. Gender differences in working patterns, in terms of shift patterns and hours worked, will also be examined. Then differences in factors relating to human capital, such as the experience of and qualifications held by male and female nurses, will be explored. Finally, given the interest of this study on differences in career progression, the extent to which gender differences in these factors vary with seniority of nurse will be explored.

While such a description is an important part of understanding gender differences in career progression, it must be recognised that the data presented in this chapter are descriptive and therefore do not provide an explanation for any of the patterns described. Such an explanatory focus will be found in Chapter 5.

TYPE OF NURSE, GRADE AND SPECIALITY

Once the survey sample had been weighted to account for the sampling strategy adopted (see Chapter 1), 7.2 per cent of the respondents were men. The survey covered both qualified and unqualified staff, nurses in grades A to I, and nurses working in a variety of specialities.

Table 2.1 shows the basic nursing qualifications held by women and men. Men were slightly less likely to be in unqualified nursing positions and much less likely to be enrolled nurses than women. If qualified nurses only are considered, almost 18 per cent of women were enrolled nurses compared to just over 11 per cent of men, making

Table 2.1 Basic nursing qualifications

		column percentages
	Women	*Men*
Type of nurse		
Unqualified	23	18
Enrolled	14	9
Registered	63	72
Weighted base	*13185*	*1028*
Unweighted base	*13139*	*1058*

qualified female nurses more than 50 per cent more likely than men to be enrolled.

Table 2.2 considers the distribution of men and women across nursing grades for the three types of nurse. For registered nurses the pattern is not entirely clear. If the chances of being a grade F or above or a grade G or above are considered, there were no differences between men and women. However, men were 80 per cent more likely to be a grade H or above (a statistically significant difference) and more than three times more likely to be a grade I. The differences for enrolled and unqualified nurses were clearer. Men were much less likely to be in the more junior grades and much more likely to be in the more senior grades – about 60 per cent more likely in both cases. Overall then, there

Table 2.2 Distribution of men and women across nursing grades

						column percentages
	Registered nurses		*Enrolled nurses*		*Unqualified nurses*	
	Women	*Men*	*Women*	*Men*	*Women*	*Men*
Grade						
A	–	–	–	–	81	70
B	–	–	–	–	19	30
C	–	–	22	10	–	–
D	16	20	60	60	–	–
E	32	29	18	30	–	–
F	17	14	–	–	–	–
G	29	26	–	–	–	–
H	5	6	–	–	–	–
I	2	6	–	–	–	–
Weighted base	*8333*	*731*	*1803*	*96*	*2989*	*188*
Unweighted base	*8423*	*757*	*1754*	*98*	*2907*	*190*

Table 2.3 Specialities worked in

column percentages

	Registered nurses		Enrolled nurses		Unqualified nurses	
	Women	*Men*	*Women*	*Men*	*Women*	*Men*
Speciality						
Medical or surgical	41	36	52	41	34	20
Obstetrics or gynaecology	15	1	4	1	9	0
Paediatrics	5	3	6	1	5	0
Geriatrics	8	10	17	6	29	18
Mental illness or handicap	6	48	8	50	16	60
Community	25	2	13	1	7	2
Weighted base	8170	719	1792	96	2838	180
Unweighted base	8263	744	1741	98	2757	184

appears to have been a consistent pattern, men were more likely to be in the most senior grades across all three types of nurse.

Table 2.3 considers the specialities worked in by women and men. Across all three types of nurse there were some common patterns. Men were much less likely to work in obstetrics or gynaecology, paediatrics, and in the community, and much more likely to work in mental illness or handicap. The pattern was not quite so consistent for geriatrics, where registered men and women were just as likely to work, but where enrolled and unqualified women were more likely than equivalent men to work. It is also interesting to note that unqualified staff were more likely than enrolled staff, and in turn, enrolled staff were more likely than registered staff, to be working in geriatrics. The opposite was the case for community jobs, which were mainly filled by female registered nurses. Respondents were also asked about the type of community job they did. As Table 2.3 shows, very few men were actually working in the community, so it was not possible to draw firm conclusions about gender differences here. However, it appears that the majority of men working in the community worked as district or practice nurses, while almost a quarter of female registered nurses in the community were health visitors.

SHIFT PATTERNS AND HOURS OF WORK

The various shifts worked by nurses in the NHS were grouped into the four broad categories used in Table 2.4, which shows the shifts worked by nurses and their preferred shift pattern. Overall, just over half of

Table 2.4 Shift patterns

column percentages, multiple response

	Present shift		Preferred shift	
	Women	*Men*	*Women*	*Men*
Rotating				
Earlies, lates and nights	26	39	16	24
Earlies and lates	25	25	20	23
Days Only				
Days 9–5	23	22	22	23
Days 9–3	2	0	9	2
Earlies Only	2	*	4	2
Lates and Evenings				
Nights	16	9	14	10
Lates only	*	*	1	*
Evenings	2	*	1	*
Other				
Split shift	1	1	1	1
Flexi	2	3	12	14
Other	4	2	3	3
Weighted base	13,243	1,035	12,948	1,024
Unweighted base	13,202	1,066	12,911	1,055

*< 0.5 per cent

the respondents rotated through the different shifts, while a quarter were working only during the day, 15 per cent were working only during the night, and the remainder were working to some other arrangements. Men were more likely than women to work a mix of earlies, lates and nights and more women than men worked nights only. We can see that these patterns of work approximated to individual preferences, although differences between actual and preferred shift patterns did exist. Only 2 per cent of nursing staff, for example, were working flexible hours but 12 per cent of women and 14 per cent of men said they would prefer to. It is also interesting to note that men were more likely to prefer working rotating shifts, while women were more likely to prefer working the part-time 9am to 3pm shift.

Not shown in the table is that registered nurses were more likely to be working regular 9 to 5 shifts than enrolled or unqualified nursing staff and less likely to be working nights. Again, this appears to tie in with preferences. A larger proportion of registered nurses said they would prefer to work flexible hours than unqualified nursing staff, although five times as many registered nurses would prefer to work flexible hours than were actually doing so.

Table 2.5 Part- and full-time working

column percentages

	Registered nurses		Enrolled nurses		Unqualified nurses	
	Women	*Men*	*Women*	*Men*	*Women*	*Men*
Hours worked						
35 plus	62	97	43	90	36	91
24 to 34	14	2	23	5	32	6
Less than 24	23	2	34	5	32	3
Weighted base	8322	738	1802	96	2958	188
Unweighted base	8404	762	1751	98	2881	190

In the labour market as a whole, 44 per cent of all women say that they work part-time and 63 per cent of women with dependent children say that they do so, compared with only 8 per cent of men (Sly *et al.*, 1997). Table 2.5 looks at gender differences in part-time working among nursing staff. The pattern for female enrolled and unqualified nurses was broadly similar, almost two-thirds of them worked part-time (less than 35 hours per week) and around a third of them worked less than 24 hours a week. In contrast, almost two-thirds of female registered nurses worked full-time, with just under a quarter working less than 24 hours per week. Not surprisingly, very few of the male nurses (just over 5 per cent altogether) worked part-time, although rates were lower for registered male nurses and higher for enrolled and unqualified male nurses.

AGE, ETHNICITY, YEARS IN NURSING AND QUALIFICATIONS

In a cross-sectional survey such as this there are a number of explanations relating to differences in human capital that may account for any differences shown in the position of men and women. Differences in the age profile of male and female nurses are considered in Table 2.6. This shows only one difference among registered nurses – women were significantly more likely to be aged 50 or older, while men were more likely to be in the 40 to 49 year-old age group. For enrolled nurses men were more likely to be in the 40 or older age groups, while women were more likely to be in their 30s. Among unqualified nurses there were clearer differences, men had a much younger age profile than women.

A previous report on this study showed that ethnicity has an influence on career progression in nursing, with ethnic minority nurses, particularly black nurses, not doing as well as white nurses (Beishon *et al.*, 1995). Table 2.7 explores the relationship between ethnicity and

Table 2.6 Age

column percentages

	Registered nurses		Enrolled nurses		Unqualified nurses	
	Women	Men	Women	Men	Women	Men
Age						
Below 25	4	3	-	-	6	13
25 to 29	16	18	9	8	8	14
30 to 39	35	35	42	32	18	29
40 to 49	26	33	30	38	31	24
50 or older	19	11	18	22	36	20
Mean age	39	38	41	43	44	39
Weighted base	8300	737	1788	96	2973	188
Unweighted base	8387	762	1730	98	2890	191

gender among the three types of nurse and for four ethnic groups: whites (including Irish and Europeans); Caribbean or black; South Asian (Indians, Pakistanis, Bangladeshis, Sri Lankans and Mauritians); and others (including Chinese). For all groups of nurse, men were much more likely to describe themselves as either South Asian or as one of the 'other' categories and this difference was statistically significant. Indeed, for both enrolled and registered nurses the chance of men being South Asian was five times greater than that for women. Male registered nurses were also more likely to be Caribbean or black. (Differences here for enrolled and unqualified nurses were small and not statistically significant.)

It is also possible that grade differences between men and women were a result of differences in the time they had spent in nursing. Table 2.8 explores the time since entry into the nursing profession and shows slightly different results for the two groups of qualified nurses. Among

Table 2.7 Ethnicity

column percentages

	Registered nurses		Enrolled nurses		Unqualified nurses	
	Women	Men	Women	Men	Women	Men
Ethnic group						
White	93	79	87	77	92	87
Caribbean or black	4	7	8	6	6	7
South Asian	2	10	2	11	1	4
Other	2	4	2	6	1	2
Weighted base	7750	701	1709	92	2732	180
Unweighted base	7890	732	1669	93	2673	184

Table 2.8 Years since qualification as a nurse or began nursing if unqualified

column percentages

	Registered nurses		Enrolled nurses		Unqualified nurses	
	Women	*Men*	*Women*	*Men*	*Women*	*Men*
Years since began nursing						
2 or less	5	11	-	-	9	28
3 to 5	10	14	4	4	16	25
6 to 10	20	20	18	16	22	28
11 to 15	18	16	24	13	18	10
16 to 20	13	17	22	21	15	4
More than 20	34	23	31	45	19	4
Weighted base	*8290*	*737*	*1791*	*96*	*2943*	*185*
Unweighted base	*8372*	*760*	*1738*	*98*	*2863*	*189*

registered nurses, women had on average been qualified longer than men; men were twice as likely to have been qualified for two years or less and women were one and a half times more likely to have been qualified for more than twenty years. However, for enrolled nurses men were one and a half times more likely than women to have been qualified for more than 20 years. Among unqualified nurses the pattern is similar to, but more striking than that for registered nurses. Men were much more likely to have first entered nursing five or fewer years ago and much less likely to have been nursing for more than ten years. Very few men had begun nursing more than 20 years ago.

Of course differences in time spent since entry into nursing do not account for the possibly greater time female nurses may have spent out of the workforce compared with men. Gender differences in taking career breaks, including the reasons for taking breaks and the length of

Table 2.9 Years spent working as a nurse

column percentages

	Registered nurses		Enrolled nurses		Unqualified nurses	
	Women	*Men*	*Women*	*Men*	*Women*	*Men*
Years working as a nurse						
2 or less	4	6	4	4	26	37
3 to 5	7	14	2	1	16	21
6 to 10	23	25	17	17	20	28
11 to 15	21	16	27	17	15	9
16 to 20	16	15	23	19	14	3
More than 20	28	25	26	42	10	3
Weighted base	*8315*	*739*	*1805*	*96*	*3008*	*190*
Unweighted base	*8401*	*765*	*1755*	*98*	*2927*	*193*

Table 2.10 Qualifications above minimum requirement held by enrolled and registered nurses

column percentages

	Registered nurses		Enrolled nurses	
	Women	*Men*	*Women*	*Men*
Qualifications excluding those related to nursing				
5 O-levels or equivalent	min	min	14	3
A-level or equivalent	26	24	8	6
Diploma or equivalent	13	20	3	3
Degree or equivalent	2	7	0	1
Additional nursing qualifications beyond registration/enrollment				
Certificate	4	2	1	2
Diploma	15	6	4	1
Degree	3	3	0	0
All qualifications – including nursing diplomas and degrees				
A-level/diploma or equivalent	45	45	14	10
Degree or equivalent	5	10	0	1
Weighted base	*8364*	*742*	*1811*	*96*
Unweighted base	*8450*	*767*	*1760*	*98*

breaks, are discussed in full in Chapter 4. Here, to give a more direct indication of experience working as a nurse Table 2.9 shows the number of years spent actually nursing. In contrast to Table 2.8, it shows few differences between female and male registered nurses, though men had, on the whole, worked slightly fewer years than women. However, the pattern for enrolled and unqualified nurses remains much the same in Table 2.9 as in Table 2.8 – enrolled men were again one and a half times more likely than enrolled women to have 20 or more years experience and, in contrast, unqualified men were more likely to have worked for five or less years and less likely to have worked for ten or more years than unqualified women.

Differences in qualifications on entry into nursing and additional qualifications obtained once initial training had been completed could also produce a different career outcome for male and female nurses. Table 2.10 considers this for qualified nurses. For registered nurses there appears to be two contradictory findings. If 'non-nursing' qualifications are considered (the first part of the table), men appear to have been better qualified than women – they were 70 per cent more likely to have qualifications that were better than A-level and this difference was statistically significant. These were likely, but not certain, to have been

Table 2.11 Training and career development – qualified nurses only

column percentages

	Registered nurses		Enrolled nurses	
	Women	Men	Women	Men
Ease of access to information on courses				
Very/fairly easy	58	60	38	38
Neither	17	20	19	28
Very/fairly difficult	25	20	43	34
Weighted base	*8188*	*727*	*1749*	*95*
Unweighted base	*8271*	*754*	*1693*	*96*
Ease of getting paid time off				
Very/fairly easy	27	31	25	29
Neither	16	23	16	23
Very/fairly difficult	57	46	59	49
Weighted base	*8174*	*729*	*1741*	*94*
Unweighted base	*8259*	*755*	*1687*	*96*

qualifications obtained prior to entry into nurse training. However, men were less likely to have obtained nursing qualifications after they had qualified as a nurse (the middle part of the table) – women were more than twice as likely to have obtained a nursing diploma and this difference was also statistically significant. If any of the qualifications the respondents held by the time they completed the questionnaire are considered (the final part of the table), differences only remain for men and women at degree level and, as the earlier parts of the table showed, this was only present for non-nursing degrees.

EXPECTATIONS OF EASE OF ACCESS TO TRAINING OPPORTUNITIES AND CAREER DEVELOPMENT

When considering human capital differences between men and women in nursing, access to training and career development is an important factor. Both qualified and unqualified nursing staff were asked about their expectations concerning ease of access to training opportunities. Tables 2.11 and 2.12 show the responses for qualified nursing staff only, unqualified staff are discussed after this. In terms of getting access to information on courses, there were few differences between men and women, although women were slightly more likely to say that this was difficult (differences were statistically significant for registered nurses). However, while about 60 per cent of registered nurses reported that it was easy for them to get access to information on courses, this was the case for only about two-fifths of the enrolled nurses. The second half of

Table 2.12 Encouragement to take post-basic training – qualified nurses only

column percentages

	Registered nurses		Enrolled nurses	
	Women	*Men*	*Women*	*Men*
Encouragement to take courses				
Encourages a lot	17	19	13	14
Encourages a bit	27	28	19	20
Neither	42	38	54	51
Discourages a bit	8	10	7	7
Discourages a lot	5	5	7	8
Weighted base	*8168*	*727*	*1730*	*93*
Unweighted base	*8252*	*753*	*1677*	*95*

the table shows that there was a statistically significant difference between male and female nurses in their perceptions of the ease with which they would get access to paid time off to go on courses – 57 per cent of female registered nurses compared with 46 per cent of male registered nurses thought it would be difficult to get paid study leave and a similar difference was present for enrolled nurses. In addition, not shown in the table is that around 60 per cent of qualified nursing staff expected to have difficulties in getting their course fees paid, but there were few differences in this between male and female nurses.

Table 2.12 shows the extent to which qualified staff felt that they had been encouraged to take post-basic training. There were marginal differences between male and female nurses regardless of type of nurse. However, there were large differences between registered and enrolled nursing staff: enrolled nurses reported receiving much less encourage-

Table 2.13 Age – registered nurses only

column percentages

	D to G grade nurses		H or I grade nurses	
	Women	*Men*	*Women*	*Men*
Age				
Below 25	4	4	–	–
25 to 29	17	21	1	1
30 to 39	36	36	26	34
40 to 49	25	30	35	47
50 or older	17	9	37	19
Mean age	*39*	*37*	*46*	*43*
Weighted base	*7705*	*638*	*564*	*88*
Unweighted base	*7734*	*664*	*626*	*88*

Table 2.14 Years since qualification – registered nurses only

column percentages

	D to G grade nurses		H or I grade nurses	
	Women	*Men*	*Women*	*Men*
Years since qualified				
5 or less	17	28	–	–
6 to 10	21	21	7	10
11 to 15	18	17	14	15
16 to 20	13	16	16	22
More than 20	32	18	62	53
Weighted base	7699	638	561	88
Unweighted base	7723	662	623	88

ment to go on further training courses than registered staff. It is worrying to note that a significant minority, about 14 per cent, of nurses reported that they were actually discouraged from taking further training.

Interestingly, while a similar proportion of male and female enrolled nurses – about 48 per cent – had applied for a conversion course to become a registered nurse at some point in their career, a greater proportion of male enrolled nurses said that they intended to apply for a conversion course in the next 12 months – 53 per cent compared with 40 per cent of female enrolled nurses, a statistically significant difference.

Auxiliary and unqualified nursing staff were also asked about their development within the NHS. More unqualified male nursing staff (31 per cent) had applied to undertake basic nurse training than female staff (22 per cent) and this difference was statistically significant. In addition, significantly more men than women said that they had been encouraged to go on further training courses – 43 per cent of unqualified male staff said they had been encouraged to take further training compared with 35 per cent of female unqualified staff. Unqualified male members of staff also felt that they would find it easier to get their course fees paid than equivalent females – 28 per cent of unqualified male staff said it would be easy to get their course fees paid compared with 21 per cent of unqualified female staff and again this difference was statistically significant.

DIFFERENCES BETWEEN SENIOR AND JUNIOR NURSES

Important differences between the male and female respondents to the survey have begun to emerge throughout the tables shown so far. However, in terms of career success, the central difference was that

Table 2.15 Speciality worked in – registered nurses only

column percentages

	D to G grade nurses		H or I grade nurses	
	Women	*Men*	*Women*	*Men*
Speciality				
Medical or surgical	41	37	37	28
Obstetrics or gynaecology	16	1	10	0
Paediatrics	6	3	4	4
Geriatrics	8	10	4	6
Mental illness or handicap	6	47	6	55
Community	24	2	40	7
Weighted base	7630	629	514	81
Unweighted base	7666	654	574	81

shown in Table 2.2, where male nurses were more likely to be in senior grades for all three types of nurse. For registered nurses differences appeared to emerge above grade G – men were almost twice as likely as women to be above grade G. This suggests that it might be worth considering whether differences between male and female registered nurses remain regardless of seniority and whether senior registered female nurses (those in grade H or I positions) are different from those who are more junior.

Age differences for registered nurses are shown in Table 2.13, which demonstrates that the younger age profile of male registered nurses (see Table 2.6) was also present among those who had reached

Table 2.16 Qualifications above minimum requirement held by registered nurses

column percentages

	D to G grade nurses		H or I grade nurses	
	Women	*Men*	*Women*	*Men*
Qualifications excluding those related to nursing				
A-level or equivalent	27	25	19	19
Diploma or equivalent	12	18	31	34
Degree or equivalent	2	7	5	4
Additional nursing qualifications				
Certificate	4	2	3	2
Diploma	13	5	40	15
Degree	3	3	7	6
Weighted base	7768	643	565	88
Unweighted base	7795	669	628	88

Table 2.17 Part- and full-time working for registered nurses

column percentages

	D to G grade nurses		H or I grade nurses	
	Women	*Men*	*Women*	*Men*
Hours worked				
35 plus	61	96	87	100
24 to 34	15	2	7	0
Less than 24	25	2	6	0
Weighted base	7728	639	563	88
Unweighted base	7752	664	626	88

grades H and I. For both senior (H or I grade) and junior (those below H grade) nurses, women were twice as likely to be aged 50 or older. Table 2.14 looks at differences in time since qualification and shows that, while differences were present for the more junior nurses – with female registered nurses below H grade being more likely than their male equivalents to have been qualified for more than 20 years – differences for male and female H and I grade nurses were small and not statistically significant.

Table 2.15 considers speciality worked in. This shows a similar pattern to that found in Table 2.3, women were much more likely to be in community jobs and men were much more likely to be in mental illness or handicap jobs, regardless of grade. However, female grade H and I registered nurses were also much more likely than their more junior counterparts to work in the community and this difference was statistically significant. This suggests that particular specialities offer more opportunities for promotion for female nurses.

Table 2.16 considers the qualifications held by registered nurses. While male nurses below H or I grade were more likely than equivalent female nurses to have non-nursing qualifications above A-level, this was not the case for the more senior nurses, who had similar non-nursing qualifications regardless of gender. If nursing qualifications are considered, however, female H and I grade nurses were considerably better qualified than their male counterparts: they were more than two and half times more likely to have obtained a nursing diploma. Although nurses below H and I grade were less likely to have additional nursing qualifications, a similar gender difference was present.

Table 2.17 looks at hours of work for registered nursing staff. This shows that senior female registered nurses were considerably less likely than their counterparts below grade H to be part-time workers (i.e. to work less than 35 hours per week), although they were still more likely than men to work part-time. In fact, none of the senior male registered nurses in our sample worked part-time.

CONCLUSION

In this descriptive examination of the job-related differences between male and female nurses, important patterns have already emerged. Male nurses were, on the whole, younger than their female counterparts and more likely to be from an ethnic minority background. Female nurses had been, on the whole, qualified for longer and were more likely to have gained additional nursing qualifications beyond their initial registration/enrollment. Male nurses were less likely to be enrolled, men and women were concentrated in different specialities (women were more likely than men to work in obstetrics, gynaecology and the community, while men were more likely to work in mental illness and handicap) and women were more likely to work part-time and to work night shifts. Most important, though, was the findings that for all three types of nurse considered (registered, enrolled and unqualified), male nurses were much more likely to be in senior grades (see Table 2.2).

In order to further examine this difference in the proportion of men and women in senior grades, the final section of this chapter explored whether the differences in the position of men and women in nursing described in earlier tables were consistent across senior (H or I) and junior (below H) grades for registered nurses. Almost all of the differences between men and women remained even after taking seniority of grade into account. However, while men below H grade had been qualified for a shorter period than their female counterparts, this was not the case for male and female nurses who were in H or I grade positions, and gender differences in the rate of part-time working were also diminished for this group (although they were still present).

As explained in the introduction, the emphasis in this chapter has been on description rather than explanation. The next two chapters will begin exploring possible reasons for some of the differences outlined so far in this chapter, in particular the degree to which they might be a consequence of differences in the attitudes and expectations of male and female staff, and how far they might be a consequence of the often greater domestic responsibilities that women face.

CHAPTER 3

Perceptions, Attitudes and Expectations of Nursing Staff

INTRODUCTION

In the previous chapter, we explored how far the 'human capital' explanations that may account for any gender differences in career progression, varied across male and female nurses. In addition to these factors, the wider literature on women and employment has highlighted the importance of more subjective issues that concern perceptions, attitudes and expectations – such as differences in labour market orientation and perceived gender roles. Hakim (1995), for example, has contended that some women may be less orientated to career success than men and more 'home-centred'. There is some evidence to support such a hypothesis within the nursing profession. One study found that men were more likely than women to expect promotion (Waite and Hutt, 1987) and other large scale surveys have suggested that female nurses are less interested than males in promotion or the prospect of working in management (Rogers, 1983, Price Waterhouse, 1988). A smaller study suggested that men were more likely to have entered nursing because of its opportunities and challenges and to say that they wanted promotion, while both male and female nurses felt that men were more ambitious (Skevington and Dawkes, 1988). Of course, the fact that women were less likely to expect promotion may have been a reflection of a realistic appraisal of their chances, which might also have led to their lower ambition and interest in promotion. In this context it is interesting to note that Davies and Rosser's (1986) work suggests that women are just as likely as men to be committed to nursing work and professional development.

This chapter provides a descriptive analysis of the attitudes and expectations of male and female nursing staff in the NHS. The focus will be on: gender differences in reasons for entering nursing; career-orientation; satisfaction with current grade; areas of dissatisfaction with work; and expectations for future career development.

REASONS FOR ENTERING NURSING

An investigation of men and women's initial motivations to enter the nursing profession provides one way of assessing gender differences in career orientation. In this survey, respondents were asked how important various factors were to them in deciding to enter nursing. Table 3.1 gives an overall ranking of these factors for all nursing staff, based on those factors that they said had been 'very important' to them. Aspects of work relating to what we have called 'personal fulfilment', such as having rewarding, interesting and varied work, appeared to be the most important factors in determining entry into nursing. In addition, three-fifths of nursing staff reported that the quality of initial training and security of employment had also been very important to them. Interestingly, pay and promotion were of considerably less importance than these factors to nurses on entry into the profession.

Using a factor analysis[7] approach, three main dimensions among these reasons for entering nursing were identified. These were 'personal fulfilment', 'career opportunities' and 'pay and conditions'. Table 3.2 again looks at the proportion of respondents who said that particular items were 'very important' reasons for entering nursing, and shows the importance of these three dimensions and their component parts separately for men and women and for type of nurse.

A greater proportion of female nurses said that factors relating to personal fulfilment had been very important to them in determining entry into nursing compared with male nurses. However, as for women, this was the most common factor reported by men as very important. Although the career opportunities available in nursing were less frequently reported as very important for all nursing staff, men were more likely than women to have reported that promotion and career structure were very important to them, and these differences were statistically significant. Across all three types of nurse, 36 per cent of men said that the prospect of promotion had been very important to their decision to enter nursing, compared with 29 per cent of women, and there was a similar, but slightly smaller, gender difference in those saying that the prospect of a career structure had been very important – 35 per cent of men and 30 per cent of women. Female nursing staff were more likely than male staff to say the quality of initial training and the prospect of further training had been very important to them and these differences were also statistically significant. For both men and women, 'pay and conditions' were just as likely as 'career oppor-

7. Factor analysis is an analytical tool that enables us to identify the chief underlying dimensions of a set of identified attributes or responses to a series of questions (Oppenheim, 1992: 166).

Table 3.1 Reasons for entering nursing or nursing auxiliary work

	Per cent rating factor 'very important'
Rewarding work	86
Interesting work	83
Variety of work	75
Quality of initial training	60
Security of employment	59
A job suiting your talents	54
Helping others in the community	53
Prospects of further training	51
Plenty of jobs likely to be available	37
Prospects of a career structure	30
Prospects of promotion	29
Long-term salary prospects	27
Opportunities to take responsibility	26
Flexibility of hours of work	22
Status of the job	22
Opportunities to give supervision	18
Starting salary	13
Family member or friend in nursing	10
Opportunities to travel	5
Other reason	5
Weighted base	*13,698*
Unweighted base	*13,691*

tunities' to have been reported as very important in choosing to enter nursing. However, men were more likely than women to have reported that their longer term salary prospects were very important, while women were more likely to have identified flexibility of working hours as very important.

Table 3.2 also shows that there were differences in the relative importance of these three sets of factors in determining entry into nursing between the different types of nurse. Those items relating to personal fulfilment remained the most likely to be reported as very important, regardless of type of nurse. However, while about two-thirds of enrolled and unqualified nurses reported that job security was also a very important factor in determining their entry into nursing, only a little over half of the female registered nurses reported this. In addition, unqualified nursing staff, especially women, were far more likely than registered nurses to have entered nursing because of its pay and conditions. Particularly important here was their initial pay. A similar, but smaller, difference was present for enrolled nurses, who also attached greater importance to their pay than registered nurses. These differences in the reported importance of pay and conditions across the three types of nurse may have been a consequence of

Table 3.2 Reason for entering nursing by type of nurse

per cent rating factor 'very important'

	Registered nurses		Enrolled nurses		Unqualified nurses	
	Women	*Men*	*Women*	*Men*	*Women*	*Men*
Personal Fulfilment						
Rewarding work	88	73	89	68	85	72
Interesting work	86	72	84	71	78	76
Variety of work	81	61	75	52	66	61
Career Opportunities						
Initial training	66	40	65	52	46	37
Further training	56	46	50	47	39	45
Lots of jobs	39	35	40	34	31	30
Career structure	34	37	26	33	20	28
Promotion	36	41	21	28	15	21
Responsibility	28	33	21	22	20	25
Status	22	17	23	12	22	21
Supervision	21	22	17	23	11	12
Travel	6	7	3	3	2	5
Pay and conditions						
Job security	55	62	65	71	67	67
Long-term salary	22	30	31	38	39	42
Flexible hours	15	13	28	14	40	32
Starting salary	7	10	13	22	29	25
Other						
Suited talents	55	45	52	47	57	51
Help community	48	44	61	56	65	53
Family/friends	9	13	10	13	12	15
Other	5	7	5	3	5	12
Weighted base	8036	712	1736	95	2855	173
Unweighted base	8121	736	1685	95	2776	173

differences in their employment prospects outside of the nursing profession. Nevertheless, it is worth emphasising that for both enrolled and unqualified nurses, non-instrumental rewards relating to personal fulfilment were far more likely than pay to have been reported as very important reasons for entering nursing. Registered nursing staff were more likely than enrolled nurses to say that their prospects for promotion and career development had been very important in determining their entry into nursing – 41 per cent of registered male nurses and 36 per cent of registered female nurses said that the prospects of promotion had been very important, compared with 28 and 21 per cent of enrolled male and female nursing staff respectively.

Looking at gender differences within each type of nurse showed a consistent pattern along the lines of that outlined above. Slightly more women placed importance on factors relating to personal fulfilment and men were more likely to say that factors relating to career opportunities had been very important to them. Interestingly, two-thirds of female registered and enrolled nurses, but only between two-fifths and a half of male registered and enrolled nurses reported that the initial training had been very important in influencing their decision to enter nursing. This may have been a reflection of differences in the qualifications held by male and female nurses on entry into nursing (see Table 2.10). Interestingly, Table 2.10 also shows that once they had qualified as a nurse, women were far more likely than men to have taken up training opportunities and to have gained additional nursing qualifications.

Despite the gender differences that exist in Table 3.2, overall the biggest differences in motivation to enter the nursing profession were present between types of nursing staff rather than between men and women.

CAREER ORIENTATION

As described above, one hypothesis for the difference in the position of men and women in nursing is that some women may be less orientated to career success (Rogers, 1983; Hakim, 1995). From the above analysis of attitudinal data, it appears that there were minor differences in male and female motivations for entering the nursing profession, with male staff placing greater importance on some components of the career factor. Although we were not able to assess overall career orientation and ambition directly from the data we had available, in order to explore this further we used these attitudinal data to construct a scale to measure career orientation on entry into nursing. Such a combination of several but related aspects of a single underlying dimension should provide a more accurate differentiation between nursing staff in a single measure than a reliance on the individual items. Therefore, a ten-point index (lowest = 0, highest = 9) of relative career orientation was constructed.[8] One point was added to the scale for each of the following reasons that the respondent said had been *very important* to her or him in deciding to enter nursing or nursing auxiliary work:

1. Prospects of promotion.
2. Opportunities to take responsibility.
3. Opportunities to give supervision.
4. Prospects of further training.
5. Prospects of a career structure.

8. The scale was constructed from the 'career' factors identified in the factor analysis (see Table 3.2). 'Opportunities to travel' was dropped from the scale and 'long-term salary prospects' added to improve the face validity and internal reliability of the scale. The scale had a high degree of internal reliability with a Cronbach alpha coefficient of 0.84.

6. Quality of initial training.
7. Status of the job.
8. Plenty of jobs likely to be available.
9. Long-term salary prospects.

Obviously career motivations may change over time, but we felt that it was unlikely that an item that was described as initially being very important in determining entry into nursing would currently be of little importance. Thus, we felt it reasonable, though not ideal, to use initial motivations for entering nursing as a proxy for career orientation.[9]

This attitudinal scaling technique allows each respondent to be placed on a continuum in relation to other nursing staff in relative, but not absolute, terms. That is, a score of four on the relative career orientation scale indicates that orientation was higher than a score of two, but not necessarily twice as high. As a rule of thumb, we took a score of three or more on the scale to indicate a 'high' career orientation.

Table 3.3 provides the comparison of career orientation between male and female unqualified, enrolled and registered nursing staff. What is striking about this table is the remarkably similar distribution of men and women across the measure. There was little difference in the proportion of male and female nursing staff scoring three or more points on the scale (indicating a 'high' career orientation) within each nursing type, and even if finer divisions on the scale are used, differences between men and women were minimal. However, as might be expected, qualified nurses were significantly more career orientated than unqualified staff. In contrast to this, it is interesting to note that an examination of responses from registered nurses by grade showed that there was no difference between those in senior (H or I) and junior (below H) nursing grades. That is, junior nursing staff appeared to be as career orientated as more senior nurses.

Table 3.3, consequently, leads to an important conclusion. Although there was some variation in response to individual items in the career orientation measure (in particular, men placed a greater importance on the prospect of promotion when entering the nursing profession (see Table 3.2)), when the relevant indicators were combined using our attitudinal scaling technique, *there was no significant difference in overall career orientation between male and female nursing staff.*

In order to explore gender differences in motivations for entering

---

9. Career orientation might well have changed following entry into nursing. While it would have been useful to have had data that looked at this, it is important to recognise that any changes in career orientation that might have occurred could well have been a result of work experiences, so it would have been impossible to determine whether current orientation was a consequence or cause of the degree of career progression experienced.

Table 3.3 Career orientation scale

column percentages

	Registered nurses		Enrolled nurses		Unqualified nurses	
	Women	*Men*	*Women*	*Men*	*Women*	*Men*
Score						
0	18	21	19	23	30	32
1	14	15	16	15	18	14
2	15	13	17	11	14	14
3	13	15	15	15	11	13
4	11	10	11	10	9	10
5	9	7	8	9	6	4
6	8	7	6	3	5	5
7	5	5	4	10	4	3
8	3	3	2	2	2	2
9	2	3	3	2	1	3
Mean	3.1	2.9	2.8	2.9	2.3	2.4
% scoring 3+	53	50	48	50	38	41
Weighted base	8364	742	1811	96	3010	190
Unweighted base	8450	767	1760	98	2929	193

nursing further, two additional scales were produced. These were based on the other factors identified as underlying reasons for entering the nursing profession in Table 3.2, namely 'personal fulfilment' and 'pay and conditions'.

The personal fulfilment scale is a four-point index (lowest = 0, highest = 3). One point was added to the scale[10] for each of the following that the respondent said had been very important to her or him in deciding to enter nursing or nursing auxiliary work:

1. Interesting work.
2. Rewarding work.
3. Variety of work.

The pay and conditions scale was constructed to measure the relative importance that nursing staff said that they had placed on the pay and conditions of employment when entering the nursing profession. This scale is a five-point index (lowest = 0, highest = 4). One point was added to the scale[11] for each of the following that the respondent said had been very important to her or him in deciding to enter nursing or nursing auxiliary work:

---

10. The personal fulfilment scale had satisfactory reliability with a Cronbach alpha coefficient of 0.78.
11. The pay and conditions scale also had satisfactory reliability with a Cronbach alpha coefficient of 0.77.

Table 3.4 Personal fulfilment and pay and conditions scales

	Registered nurses		Enrolled nurses		Unqualified nurses	
	Women	Men	Women	Men	Women	Men
Personal fulfilment score						
Mean	2.4	2.0	2.4	1.9	2.2	1.9
% scoring 2+	83	66	80	64	74	63
Pay and conditions score						
Mean	1.0	1.1	1.3	1.4	1.7	1.5
% scoring 2+	24	30	38	39	49	44
Weighted base	8364	742	1811	96	3010	190
Unweighted base	8450	767	1760	98	2929	193

Note: Comparisons can be made within scales but not across scales.

1. Long-term salary prospects.
2. Starting salary.
3. Flexible hours.
4. Job security.

Findings for these two scales are shown in Table 3.4. This shows that there was a statistically significant difference between male and female nursing staff in the importance they placed on personal fulfilment when entering the nursing profession. For all types of nurse, women placed a greater importance on these non-instrumental rewards than men. Although the differences were smaller for unqualified staff, this was because overall, female registered and enrolled nurses placed a greater importance on personal fulfilment than unqualified female staff, a difference that was also statistically significant. For male staff there was no such difference between types of nursing staff.

In terms of pay and conditions there was an interesting gender difference that was not consistent across type of nurse. While male registered nurses were more likely than their female counterparts to score on two or more of the relevant items (a difference that was statistically significant), this was not the case for enrolled and unqualified nurses. Table 3.2 suggests that much of this gender difference for registered nurses was a consequence of the items relating to job security and long-term salary. It is also worth noting that for both men and women a greater proportion of enrolled than registered nurses scored two or more on this scale, and a greater proportion of unqualified than enrolled nurses were in this category. Close to half of the unqualified nurses said that two or more of the pay and conditions factors had been very important to their decision to begin nursing. This difference across type of nurse may have been a consequence of the different employment opportunities they had outside nursing, as we have already pointed out.

Table 3.5 Personal fulfilment and pay and conditions scales – registered nurses only

	D to G grade nurses		H or I grade nurses	
	Women	*Men*	*Women*	*Men*
Personal fulfilment score				
Mean	2.5	2.0	2.4	2.0
% scoring 2+	83	66	81	68
Pay and conditions score				
Mean	1.0	1.1	0.8	0.8
% scoring 2+	24	22	16	24
Weighted base	7768	643	565	88
Unweighted base	7795	669	628	88

Note: Comparisons can be made within scales but not across scales.

Table 3.5 examines how far differences in the importance of personal fulfilment and pay and conditions were consistent between senior (H and I grade) and junior (below H grade) registered nurses. For personal fulfilment there was no difference between junior and senior nurses of the same gender, and the gender difference for registered nurses was present and statistically significant for both the senior and junior grades. Similarly, the gender difference in the reported importance placed on pay and conditions was present for both senior and junior grades. However, the table also shows that junior nurses were more likely than senior nurses to have reported that items relating to pay and conditions had been very important to them on entering nursing.

CURRENT GRADE AND WORKING CONDITIONS

In order to assess the extent to which there were any gender differences in satisfaction with their current working arrangements, this section focuses on responses to questions asking about the respondents' perceptions of the adequacy of their current grade and working conditions.

Respondents were asked whether they thought they undertook work that should be done by a different grade of staff. Responses to this are shown in Table 3.6. About three-quarters of all registered nursing staff believed that they did work that should be done by a lower grade on a daily or weekly basis. A slightly lower proportion, about two-thirds, of enrolled nursing staff also said this. Not surprisingly, fewer – just under a fifth – of the unqualified staff reported they did work which should be done by a lower grade. Interestingly, there was little difference between men and women in response to this question.

However, gender differences did emerge among registered nurses when respondents were asked whether they did work that should be

Table 3.6 Does work that should be done by a different grade at least weekly

cell percentages

	Registered nurses		Enrolled nurses		Unqualified nurses	
	Women	Men	Women	Men	Women	Men
Lower grade work	72	75	68	66	16	22
Higher grade work	51	67	65	64	47	61
Weighted base	*8231*	*736*	*1767*	*95*	*2735*	*181*
Unweighted base	*8315*	*759*	*1711*	*96*	*2647*	*183*

undertaken by a higher grade of staff. Table 3.6 shows that about half of the female registered nurses said they did such work on a daily or weekly basis, while this was the case for nearly two-thirds of the male staff. This was also true for unqualified nursing staff. In the case of enrolled nurses there was no difference between men and women – around two-thirds of both men and women said that they did work that ought to be done by a higher grade nurse. It is not clear whether the differences between men and women in this reflect differences in the *opportunity* to do higher grade work (which should increase the chances of promotion) or differences in the *beliefs* of men and women about the type of work they did.

Table 3.7 explores whether these differences were consistent for junior (below H grade) and senior (H or I grade) registered nurses. A greater proportion of junior registered nurses said they did work of a lower grade than senior staff and within each category, slightly more men than women said that this was the case. Similarly, more junior staff than senior staff said that they did work of a higher grade on either a daily or a weekly basis, and within each category men were more likely than women to say this.

Overall then, it appears that male staff were less satisfied with their current nursing duties than female nursing staff. Male nurses were more likely to feel that they were regularly doing work of a higher grade. In order to address this further, Table 3.8 shows responses to the

Table 3.7 Does work that should be done by a different grade at least weekly – registered nurses only

cell percentages

	D to G grade nurses		H or I grade nurses	
	Women	Men	Women	Men
Lower grade work	73	77	63	69
Higher grade work	52	71	30	41
Weighted base	*7650*	*637*	*554*	*88*
Unweighted base	*7675*	*661*	*617*	*88*

Table 3.8 Fairness of current grade

cell percentages

	Registered nurses		Enrolled nurses		Unqualified nurses	
	Women	Men	Women	Men	Women	Men
Grade not fair	36	49	46	41	61	62
Weighted base	8321	738	1786	96	2955	184
Unweighted base	8402	763	1738	97	2871	186

question that asked directly whether respondents thought that their current grading was a fair reflection of their duties and responsibilities at work.

It can be seen that a substantial proportion of nursing staff thought that their current grade was unfair. If all of the nursing staff are considered, half of the men and 43 per cent of the women felt that their current grade was not a fair reflection of their duties and responsibilities at work. A greater proportion of unqualified nursing staff, compared with registered and enrolled nurses, felt their grading was unfair. There were only small gender differences in response to this question for enrolled and unqualified nurses. However, while almost half of the male registered nurses said that their grade did not fairly reflect their duties and responsibilities, this was only the case for just over a third of female registered nurses. Exploring these differences by nursing grade for enrolled nurses showed that those who had not moved beyond grade C were far more unhappy with their current grading than those enrolled nurses who had moved further up the career ladder to grades D or E.

Among registered nurses, almost twice as many junior staff (those below H grade) than senior staff (H or I grades) – 38 per cent compared with 21 per cent respectively – felt that their current grade was unfair and this difference was statistically significant. A third of male senior registered nurses compared with a fifth of female senior staff said their grading was an unfair reflection of their work, and there were similar gender differences for junior registered nurses (51 per cent for men and 37 per cent for women).

AREAS OF (DIS)SATISFACTION

Analysis of a large random survey that contained more than 5,000 respondents in paid work, the British Household Panel Survey, revealed high levels of overall satisfaction with work among British employees – 58.7 per cent of respondents said that they were very or

Table 3.9 Overall satisfaction with current post

column percentages

	Registered nurses		Enrolled nurses		Unqualified nurses	
	Women	*Men*	*Women*	*Men*	*Women*	*Men*
Satisfied	52	36	53	48	68	49
Neither satisfied nor dissatisfied	29	34	30	32	23	30
Dissatisfied	15	24	13	14	6	16
Very dissatisfied	3	6	4	5	3	5
Weighted base	*8256*	*732*	*1779*	*92*	*2878*	*186*
Unweighted base	*8321*	*756*	*1723*	*94*	*2794*	*188*

completely satisfied with their work and almost 80 per cent said that they were at least satisfied (Clark, 1996). Respondents to the survey used here were asked how satisfied they were with their current nursing post. If all nursing staff in our survey are considered, just over half were satisfied with their work overall, a very low rate compared to Clark's (1996) findings for the general population. Men were less satisfied than women – only 39 per cent of men were satisfied overall compared with 56 per cent of female nursing staff, and this difference was consistent across type of nurse, although smaller for enrolled nurses (see Table 3.9). Unqualified nursing staff were the most satisfied overall and registered nurses were the least satisfied.

Looking solely at registered nurses, junior staff (below H grade) were less satisfied overall than senior staff (H or I grade) – 22 per cent compared with 14 per cent respectively said they were either dissatisfied or very dissatisfied. More junior male nurses were dissatisfied or very dissatisfied than equivalent female nurses (32 per cent compared with 19 per cent respectively), but there was little gender difference for senior nursing staff, although men were more likely to say that they were neither satisfied nor dissatisfied.

Clark's (1996) general population study showed similar patterns to those shown in Table 3.9, with higher levels of satisfaction both for those with lower educational attainment and for women. He proposed a number of possible explanations for the gender difference in rates of satisfaction, including: men and women may have different expectations of work; they may value work for different reasons; and they may compare their employment to different types of jobs when making a judgement of how satisfied they are. However, Clark (1996) also cited evidence suggesting that the different rates of satisfaction may be a consequence of women who are unsatisfied finding it easier than unsatisfied men to leave the work-force, so those women remaining in employment are likely to be satisfied 'survivors'. Given the concern

Table 3.10 Areas of dissatisfaction

cell percentages, 'not wholly satisfied'

| | Registered nurses | | Enrolled nurses | | Unqualified nurses | |
	Women	Men	Women	Men	Women	Men
Job Characteristics						
Training opportunity	48	46	57	53	51	47
Promotion prospects	47	57	51	46	42	57
Security	46	52	55	53	35	43
Basic pay	34	51	37	41	46	67
Decision making	33	37	31	22	28	36
Hours	25	24	23	29	20	24
Work-load and support						
Admin/clerical work	67	68	56	55	12	21
Clinical time	49	52	46	47	14	16
Work-load	44	51	43	33	32	35
Qualified support	44	51	36	30	26	33
Auxiliary support	36	43	27	40	26	31
Relationships						
Colleagues	5	5	5	2	5	9
Patients/clients	3	4	2	1	2	4
Weighted base	7575	707	1639	85	2274	161
Unweighted base	7660	729	1584	85	2230	161

with retention in nursing (Price Waterhouse, 1988) and the link between satisfaction and staying in a job (Clark, 1996), the very low rates of satisfaction within the nursing work-force, shown in Table 3.9, when compared with general population surveys must be a cause for great concern.

Respondents were asked in more detail about their satisfaction with various aspects of their work in the NHS. Factor analysis suggested that there were three underlying dimensions of satisfaction with work: 'job characteristics'; 'work-load and support' and 'relationships with colleagues and patients'. Table 3.10 gives the proportion of male and female nursing staff who were 'not wholly satisfied'[12] with various aspects of their job within each factor.

The area that both male and female nursing staff reported being least satisfied with was the amount of administration and clerical work they had to do – over half of all nursing staff were dissatisfied or very dissatisfied with this aspect of their work, but this was much more common for qualified staff, particularly registered nurses among whom two-thirds reported this as an area of dissatisfaction. In general, more men than women were dissatisfied in most areas of their work, the notable exception being the amount of training opportunities open to them. This is supported by the findings presented in Table 2.11,

---

12. 'Not wholly satisfied' is defined as either dissatisfied or very dissatisfied.

which suggested that women felt more restricted in their access to career development and in the encouragement they received to undertake further training. Despite this, men were more dissatisfied with their promotion prospects and basic pay than female nursing staff.

The area of work giving the most satisfaction to all staff was their relationships with colleagues and their patients or clients. Registered nurses were less satisfied with the amount of auxiliary and qualified support available to them than enrolled nursing staff. Again it is worrying to note that about half of all nurses were not satisfied with their training opportunities, and rates of dissatisfaction here were highest for enrolled nurses.

As previously demonstrated, a scaling technique using factor analysis allows several components of a question to be combined into a single measure. Using such an analysis of satisfaction with various aspects of work (Table 3.10), two scales were constructed to measure separately levels of dissatisfaction with 'job characteristics' and 'work-load and support'.[13]

The job characteristics scale is a seven-point index (lowest = 0, highest = 6). One point was added to the scale for each of the following aspects of work that the respondent said they were either dissatisfied or very dissatisfied with:

1. The amount of training opportunities available.
2. Promotion prospects.
3. Security of employment.
4. Basic pay.
5. Involvement in decision-making.
6. Opportunity to work the hours you want.

The work-load and support scale is a six-point index (lowest = 0, highest = 5). One point was added to the scale[14] for each of the following aspects of work that the respondent said they were not wholly satisfied with:

1. The amount of administrative/clerical work you have to do.
2. The amount of time you have for clinical nursing duties.
3. Present workload.
4. The amount of qualified nurse support available.
5. The amount of auxiliary support available.

---

13. There are only two aspects of work in the 'relationship with colleagues and patients' factor, so no scale was constructed for this factor.
14. The 'job satisfaction' scale had a Cronbach alpha coefficient of 0.73 and the 'work-load and support' scale had a Cronbach alpha coefficient of 0.77.

Table 3.11 Dissatisfaction score on job characteristics and work-load and support scales

	Registered nurses		Enrolled nurses		Unqualified nurses	
	Women	Men	Women	Men	Women	Men
Job characteristics score						
Mean	1.7	2.0	1.9	1.6	1.4	1.9
% scoring 2+	58	68	64	54	46	64
Work-load score						
Mean	1.9	2.1	1.7	1.4	0.8	1.1
% scoring 2+	61	69	54	46	24	33
Weighted base	8364	742	1811	96	3010	190
Unweighted base	8450	767	1760	98	2929	193

Note: Comparisons can be made within scales but not across scales.

Table 3.11 shows that registered and unqualified men were more likely to report dissatisfaction with these two aspects of their work than equivalent women, but that this was not the case for enrolled nurses. Registered male nurses reported the most dissatisfaction and unqualified women the least in both of these aspects of their work – nearly seven out of ten of the former scored two or more points on the work-load and support scale (indicating 'high' dissatisfaction), compared with only a quarter of the latter.

Table 3.12 looks at these factors solely for registered nurses. Dissatisfaction with job characteristics was highest among junior nurses (below H grade) and especially male junior nurses – seven out of ten of these scored at least two points on the index compared with a third of female senior registered nurses. Levels of dissatisfaction with work-load and support were more similar across senior and junior staff and male and female nurses – around six out of ten registered nurses

Table 3.12 Dissatisfaction score on job characteristics and work-load and support scales – registered nurses only

	D to G grade nurses		H or I grade nurses	
	Women	Men	Women	Men
Job characteristics score				
Mean	1.8	2.0	1.1	1.6
% Scoring 2+	60	71	35	52
Work-load score				
Mean	1.9	2.2	1.9	1.9
% Scoring 2+	61	70	62	61
Weighted base	7768	643	565	88
Unweighted base	7795	669	628	88

Note: Comparisons can be made within scales but not across scales.

scored two or more points on the scale, indicative of high levels of dissatisfaction with this aspect of the job.

THE FUTURE

Respondents were asked which of a number of things they expected to be doing in three years time. Despite the earlier tables showing the levels of dissatisfaction nurses had with certain aspects of their job and their worries about their current grading, Table 3.13 shows that over 80 per cent of nursing staff saw their future within the NHS. But there were important and statistically significant gender variations in expectations for the future. Women were more likely to say that they would be in the same job and grade in three years time, and this was particularly the case for registered nurses – 42 per cent of female registered nurses said this compared to only 28 per cent of male registered nurses. On the other hand, men were significantly more likely than women to say they would be in a *better* NHS job (in terms of their preferred speciality or higher grade) and again this was particularly the case for registered nurses – just over half of male registered nurses thought this compared with two-fifths of female registered nurses.

Overall, approximately a fifth of nursing staff thought they would be in education or raising a family in the next three years. For qualified nurses, women were much more likely than men to say that they would be raising a family, while for unqualified nurses more men thought that they would be going into education. Interestingly, of the small proportion of nurses who thought they would be in a lower grade in the near future, 15 per cent of women also said they would be raising a family, while this did not apply to any of the male nursing staff. This suggests that some female nurses were likely to anticipate a downgrading on return to work after having a family, an issue that has been documented by others (Waite *et al.*, 1989). It is also worth pointing out that, consistent with their greater levels of dissatisfaction, a larger proportion of male nursing staff thought they would be in a non-nursing job in the next three years and this was consistent across type of nurse. Interestingly, a significant minority of nursing staff thought that they would become unemployed or redundant during the next three years. This might have be due to restructuring within the NHS at the time of the survey leading to an uncertain climate.

An exploration of differences according to nursing grade among registered nurses showed that a greater proportion of junior staff (below H grade) than senior staff (H or I grade) saw themselves progressing up the career ladder to a better grade or their preferred speciality within the following three years. Again, more men than

Table 3.13 The future

column percentages, multiple response

	Registered nurses		Enrolled nurses		Unqualified nurses	
	Women	Men	Women	Men	Women	Men
Better NHS job	42	51	41	38	27	39
Same NHS job	42	28	42	40	56	32
Lower grade	5	7	5	7	1	1
Non-NHS nursing	9	15	6	11	5	13
Non-nursing	8	15	6	10	7	14
Education	11	13	9	5	5	13
Raising a family	17	6	13	2	7	6
Redundant/unemployed	7	13	9	12	8	11
Other	12	14	14	17	13	21
Weighted base	7976	722	1734	93	2745	182
Unweighted base	8061	748	1689	93	2658	184

women thought that this would be the case for both senior and junior staff. Seventeen per cent of female junior registered nurses said they would be raising a family in the next three years, compared with just 6 per cent of junior male staff. Senior female staff had a similar rate to both junior and senior male staff, which of course may have been a reflection of the age profile of female senior nurses, but perhaps also reflects differences in their chosen 'gender role' compared with more junior female nurses (Hakim, 1995).

CONCLUSION

The above analysis has highlighted some significant differences in the attitudes and expectations of male and female nursing staff. Women were more orientated than men towards non-instrumental rewards from work, such as personal fulfilment, while men were more orientated than women towards instrumental rewards, such as career opportunities. Both male and female nurses had very low levels of overall satisfaction with their work when compared with findings from general population surveys (Clark, 1996). Men were less satisfied than women with their current grade and working conditions, and were also less satisfied overall with their work. In general, male registered nurses were the least satisfied with various aspects of their work and unqualified women were the most satisfied. The area of least satisfaction for qualified nurses was the amount of administrative and clerical work they had to do. Almost half of all nurses were not satisfied with the training opportunities available to them. There were important gender variations in expectations for the future. Women were more likely to say that they would be in the same job and grade in the near future, whereas men were significantly more likely than women to say they would be in a better NHS job.

However, perhaps the most important attitudinal factor for our purposes of exploring career progression, emphasises the similarities between male and female nursing staff. Although we could not directly measure ambition or motivation from the data available, we found no significant gender differential in our proxy career-orientation scale. The implication is that the smaller proportion of female nurses who expected career progression to a higher grade or preferred speciality within the next three years compared with male nurses was not a consequence of a lesser career-orientation. Instead, it may have resulted from an anticipation of disadvantage, perhaps resulting from barriers following their greater family responsibilities. These barriers to career progression are the topic of the next chapter.

CHAPTER 4

Family Responsibilities

INTRODUCTION

The analysis so far has shown some significant differences in the position of men and women in nursing and gender differences in the perceptions and expectations of nursing staff. It is possible that these differences are accounted for by gender differences in family roles. Particularly important here may be women's greater responsibility for childcare. Of course, if such responsibilities do have an impact on the ability to undertake paid work, this will have a particular relevance to nursing, where women comprise as much as 90 per cent of the workforce (Department of Health, 1995), compared with most other occupations.

Among the key difficulties faced by women in entering employment and gaining promotion are the organisational barriers that are encountered as a result of employers' policies and practices (Callender, 1996). Employers' policies and practices may disadvantage those who are unable to comply with organisational 'norms', and this may particularly apply to women with children. The lack of part-time opportunities in management and senior posts, and the lack of flexible working conditions and childcare facilities persist, despite the increasing proportion of working mothers. Here, greater flexibility over hours and working arrangements would help employees combine their work and home commitments. When this survey was undertaken, a parallel study involving in-depth interviews with managers and staff within the NHS was also conducted (Beishon *et al.*, 1995). This included an examination of flexible working arrangements and childcare within the NHS. The findings suggested that, although there was: 'a broad commitment to flexible working arrangements amongst employers, this was clearly within the confines of the service' (Beishon *et al.*, 1995: 115). Managers felt that there was a fine balance to be struck between the needs of the employee and those of the health service.

This chapter, therefore, considers the impact of the greater family and domestic responsibilities borne by women on gender differences within nursing. Once again, it is important to bear in mind that our

Table 4.1 Children by marital status

column percentages

	Married/Cohabiting		Single	
	Women	*Men*	*Women*	*Men*
Any children under age 16				
No	54	43	82	89
Yes, all aged 6 or older	23	29	13	7
Yes, one or more aged				
less than 6	22	28	5	4
Weighted base	*10079*	*712*	*3032*	*306*
Unweighted base	*9863*	*732*	*3193*	*317*

sample is of working women and men in permanent NHS posts. It is likely that those nurses who would experience the greatest difficulties in combining family and career responsibilities will be underrepresented in our sample, because they have a greater probability of having left employment altogether.

FAMILIES WITH CHILDREN

Overall, two out of five of the sample had dependent children – about a fifth of both men and women had at least one child aged under six, and another fifth had a youngest child aged between six and fifteen. Table 4.1 looks at whether respondents reported that they had dependent children[15] by their marital status. For single women, about one in twenty had a child under the age of six, while for an additional one in eight their youngest child was aged between six and fifteen. Around 11 per cent of those with children in our sample were lone parents.[16] Fewer married/cohabiting women (45 per cent) had dependent children compared with equivalent men (57 per cent). This may be because women in our sample were older on average than the men (see Table 2.6) and therefore less likely to have children aged under 16. And, of course, a greater proportion of women who have dependent children will be absent from the labour market altogether.

There were small differences in the proportions of respondents with dependent children according to type of nurse (Table 4.2). Unqualified nursing staff were the least likely to have children under 16, and the pattern was the same for both men and women. A greater proportion of female enrolled nurses had dependent children,

---

15. In this survey, a dependent child is aged under 16.
16. National figures suggest that over a fifth of families with dependent children are headed by a lone parent. Less than a third of these parents, however, have paid jobs that involve 16 hours or more work per week (Marsh *et al.*, 1997).

Table 4.2 Children by type of nurse

column percentages

	Registered nurses		Enrolled nurses		Unqualified nurses	
	Women	*Men*	*Women*	*Men*	*Women*	*Men*
Any children under age 16?						
No	60	53	49	59	72	71
Yes, all aged 6 or older	20	24	26	23	18	17
Yes, one or more aged less than 6	20	24	25	18	10	12
Weighted base	*8350*	*741*	*1807*	*93*	*3003*	*189*
Unweighted base	*8435*	*765*	*1757*	*94*	*2920*	*192*

especially of pre-school age, compared with equivalent male staff. However, female registered nurses were less likely than male registered nurses to have children under 16 and this difference was statistically significant.

Table 4.3 focuses on registered nurses and shows that while there were no differences between senior (H and I grade) and junior (below H grade) male registered nurses, senior female nurses were much less likely to have children under 16 at home than any of the other groups. This, of course, might be a straightforward function of age (more than a third of them were aged 50 or older, compared with just 17 per cent of junior nurses (see Table 2.13)), although if that were the case a similar difference for senior men would also be expected (a fifth of senior male registered nurses were aged 50 or older, compared with just one in ten of their junior counterparts (Table 2.13)).

CAREER BREAKS

In terms of employment, one of the consequences of women's greater family responsibility is that they are more likely to take career breaks.

Table 4.3 Children – registered nurses only

column percentages

	D to G grade nurses		H or I grade nurses	
	Women	*Men*	*Women*	*Men*
Any children under age 16?				
No	59	53	72	50
Yes, all aged 6 or older	21	23	17	27
Yes, one or more aged less than 6	21	24	11	23
Weighted base	*7755*	*642*	*564*	*88*
Unweighted base	*7781*	*667*	*627*	*88*

Table 4.4 Breaks from nursing

column percentages

	Registered nurses		Enrolled nurses		Unqualified nurses	
	Women	*Men*	*Women*	*Men*	*Women*	*Men*
Number of breaks taken						
None	37	83	33	72	74	94
One	30	13	30	23	18	6
Two	22	3	25	4	6	2
Three or more	11	1	12	1	2	0
Weighted base	*8290*	*737*	*1791*	*96*	*2943*	*185*
Unweighted base	*8372*	*760*	*1738*	*98*	*2863*	*189*

This is explored in Table 4.4, which shows that for all types of nurse, women were much more likely than men to have taken one or more breaks from nursing. Particularly striking is that men who had taken one break generally had not taken another, while a large number of women had taken more than one break. Female qualified nurses were around eight times more likely than men to have taken more than one break, and more than 10 per cent of them had taken more than two breaks, compared with just one per cent of men. Not shown in the table is that the chances of taking a break were related to how long ago the respondent had qualified as a nurse or began nursing. However, differences between men and women remained statistically significant regardless of this. While only a quarter of men who had been in nursing for more than ten years had taken a break, two-thirds of women in a similar situation had taken a break. Four-fifths of women who had been in nursing for more than 20 years had taken a break.

Table 4.5 looks at the length of the longest break taken by respondents and their reasons for taking their breaks. Because of the small number of male respondents who were enrolled or unqualified and who had taken a break, figures for these nurses are not shown separately, although they are included in the 'All respondents' column. As that column suggests, throughout the table the pattern for enrolled and unqualified nurses was very similar to that for registered nurses.

The first half of Table 4.5 shows that, in addition to being more likely to take a break, women were also more likely to have taken a longer break. While not quite one in four of the men who had taken a break had done so for more than two years, this was the case for over a third women, and one in five women had taken a break for more than five years compared to one in eight of all men. The second half of the table shows the reasons given by the respondents for taking a break. The only reason that was more common for women was taking a break for having children (among which are included a very small number

Table 4.5 Length of and reasons for taking breaks – respondents who had taken at least one break

column percentages

	Registered nurses only		All respondents	
	Women	*Men*	*Women*	*Men*
Length of longest break				
One year or less	55	64	56	65
Two years	9	13	9	12
Three to five years	16	11	16	11
More than five years	20	12	19	13
*Reason for taking break**				
Children or other caring	88	7	87	9
Education	4	18	4	16
Other job	21	58	22	57
Holidays or travel	4	9	3	10
Unemployed	6	28	6	23
Ill-health	< 1	1	< 1	1
Other or not known	1	3	2	3
Weighted base	5684	182	7811	237
Unweighted base	5694	192	7767	250

* Respondent could give more than one reason

who took the break for 'caring'). About 90 per cent of the women who had taken a break had done so for this reason and women were ten times more likely than men to be in this category. Men were more likely than women to have taken the break for education, to do other types of work, to travel or go on holiday, or because they were unemployed, and these differences were statistically significant.

Among registered nurses, seniority made little difference to the chances of taking a break, with only a third of female H and I grade registered nurses saying that they had never taken a break compared to just over a third of female registered nurses below H grade. In contrast, over 80 per cent of male registered nurses regardless of grade said that they had never taken a break. There were also no differences by grade in the length of the longest break taken or the reasons for taking a break. Again, regardless of seniority almost 90 per cent of female nurses who had taken one or more breaks said that they had done so in order to have children. Of course seniority is also related to length of service, and the longer the time since qualification the greater the chance of taking a break, so a straightforward comparison such as this may have missed important differences.

Table 4.6 Part- and full-time working by marital status and type of nurse – women only

column percentages

	Registered nurses		Enrolled nurses		Unqualified nurses	
	Married/ cohabiting	Single	Married/ cohabiting	Single	Married/ cohabiting	Single
Hours worked						
35 plus	55	85	36	70	30	57
24 to 34	16	7	25	15	34	24
Less than 24	28	8	38	15	36	18
Weighted base	6278	1991	1433	351	2280	647
Unweighted base	6225	2128	1368	360	2181	659

PART-TIME WORK

Another consequence of having children for women is that they may have, or choose, to work part-time, particularly if they are single or have pre-school children. Many women with family responsibilities try to fit employment around school hours, so find part-time work more convenient.

As we saw in Chapter 2, only a little over 5 per cent of male nursing staff worked part-time (less than 35 hours per week) compared with almost two-thirds of enrolled and unqualified female nurses and just over a third of registered female nurses (Table 2.5). In order to explore part-time working among women further, Table 4.6 looks at the relationship between part-time working and marital status for the female respondents to the survey. The table shows quite clearly that marital status was related to number of hours worked for all categories of nurse – women who were single were much more likely to work full-time than those who were married or cohabiting.

Table 4.7 shows the proportion of female nursing staff working part-time by the age of their youngest child and marital status. The table shows that having children increased the chance of working part-time regardless of marital status and, in all but one case, having children aged under six increased it even further, although not by a great deal. Single mothers were less likely to work part-time than married or cohabiting mothers and the difference between married or cohabiting women and single women, shown in the first part of the table, was not a consequence of the former having children – married and cohabiting women were more likely to work part-time regardless of whether they had children or not. Registered nurses who were single and had no children were the least likely to work part-time – only 10 per cent of them did so –but they were still twice as likely as male regis-

Table 4.7 Propportion working part-time by age of child, marital status and type of nurse – women only

cell percentages

	Registered nurses		Enrolled nurses		Unqualified nurses	
	Married/ cohabiting	Single	Married/ cohabiting	Single	Married/ cohabiting	Single
No children	27	10	45	23	66	61
Children 6 to 15	60	33	76	47	79	65
Children under 6	68	50	79	54	81	(52*)
Weighted base	6278	1991	1433	351	2280	647
Unweighted base	6225	2128	1368	360	2181	659

Small cell size (<50) makes this estimate unreliable

tered nurses to work part-time and this difference was statistically significant (see Table 2.5).

Table 2.15 suggested that among registered nurses, those who were more senior (H or I grade) were much less likely than others to work part-time. However, even for senior female registered nurses part-time working was related to marital status and to having children below the age of sixteen at home. Only 5 per cent of single female H or I grade nurses without children at home worked part-time (only 1 per cent worked less than 24 hours per week), compared to more than two-fifths (43 per cent) of those female H or I grade nurses who were married or cohabiting and had children aged under six at home. In contrast, more than two-thirds (69 per cent) of female registered nurses below H grade, who were married or cohabiting and had children aged under six at home, worked part-time.

PATTERNS OF WORK

As well as part-time working and career breaks, other forms of flexible working arrangements, such as job-share, flexi-time and certain shift patterns, may benefit those nursing staff with family responsibilities. Some of the more 'family-friendly' shift patterns within the NHS are 9am to 5pm, 9am to 3pm and the night shift. In the past, the NHS offered contracts of employment for these shifts alone, but there is now a move towards rotation working, which, it has been suggested, offers greater flexibility for the employer rather than the employee (Beishon *et al.*, 1995). Table 4.8 looks in more detail at the 'days only' and 'nights only' shifts for male and female registered nurses.

Among respondents with no children, there were few gender differences in the shift pattern worked, although single women were

Table 4.8 'Family-friendly' shift patterns –registered nurses only

column percentages

	Married/Cohabiting		Single	
	Women	*Men*	*Women*	*Men*
No children				
9am–5pm	32	31	24	17
9am–3pm	1	0	1	0
Nights	8	7	5	5
Other	59	62	71	78
Weighted base	*3281*	*212*	*1655*	*174*
Unweighted base	*3293*	*218*	*1779*	*189*
Children under 6				
9am–5pm	22	29	28	*
9am–3pm	4	0	4	*
Nights	17	6	10	*
Other	57	65	59	*
Weighted base	*1564*	*167*	*105*	*7*
Unweighted base	*1558*	*168*	*113*	*8*
Children 6–15				
9am–5pm	32	36	42	*
9am–3pm	6	0	3	*
Nights	17	8	12	*
Other	45	57	42	*
Weighted base	*1453*	*163*	*239*	*13*
Unweighted base	*1396*	*162*	*245*	*16*

*Too few cases for an estimate to be made.

slightly more likely than single men to work the 9am to 5pm shift. Among those with children, however, there were important gender differences. Married or cohabiting women with pre-school children were more likely to work the part-time 9am to 3pm shift and three times more likely to work nights, compared with their male equivalents, who were more likely to work the 9am to 5pm or 'other' (predominately rotating) shifts. The proportion working night shifts was not as great among single mothers compared with married or cohabiting mothers, although still greater than the rate for men, perhaps because of the difficulty of arranging childcare other than a partner for such hours. Married or cohabiting women with school-age children were also more likely to work the part-time 9am to 3pm shift and nights, compared with their male equivalents (although only twice as likely for nights in this case). Interestingly, single women with school-age children were the most likely group to work the 9am to 5pm shift and the least likely to work the 'other' types of shifts. However, apart from this one exception, of the 'family-friendly' shifts available to nurses, only those that involved part-time or nights only work were more frequently used by women with children than men.

Table 4.9 Quality of childcare facilities – parents only

		column percentages
	Women	*Men*
How good are the facilities provided by your employer?		
Very good	3	2
Fairly good	10	11
Neither good nor bad	23	27
Fairly bad	21	20
Very bad	44	40
Weighted base	*4794*	*398*
Unweighted base	*4658*	*400*

CHILDCARE

The cost and availability of childcare is another barrier to women's labour market participation and it reduces the cash incentive to work. There is evidence that spending on childcare has been rising and this is partly because of increasing costs (Finlayson *et al.*, 1996). A recent survey on lone mothers found that a third of out-of-work lone mothers said that the cost of childcare prevented them from taking up full-time work and an additional one in eight said that they had been prevented from working by the lack of availability of childcare (Ford, 1996). Interestingly, few gave these reasons alone, suggesting that the cost and availability of childcare is of importance to parents' labour market participation in addition to the other barriers to work already mentioned. The in-depth interviews that were conducted alongside this survey also looked at childcare in the NHS. The findings from these suggested that, although some employers offered childcare facilities, the cost, availability of places and the hours of opening prevented access to many staff who would otherwise use them (Beishon *et al.*, 1995).

Of course, parents in this survey had, by definition, overcome the childcare barrier since they had remained in employment. But child-care no doubt continued to be a problem for some, both in terms of cost and because of the disruptions that would be caused by a break-down in childcare arrangements or during school holidays, for example. Parents were asked how good they felt the childcare facilities offered by their employer were (although they were not asked whether any childcare facilities actually existed). Table 4.9 shows that just 13 per cent of respondents with children felt that the childcare arrange-ments offered by their employer were good, as many as two-thirds thought they were bad and close to half thought they were very bad. It is not possible to tell whether respondents reported facilities as bad because none existed.

CONCLUSION

Central to any investigation of gender differences in employment is women's greater household and family responsibilities. Two out of five nursing staff had dependent children under the age of 16. Women were considerably more likely than men to have taken at least one career break and were also more likely to have taken a longer break. In addition, women were ten times more likely than men to have taken a career break to have children. We showed earlier that women were significantly more likely than men to be working part-time regardless of seniority or nurse type. Being married or cohabiting and having dependent children further increased their chances of working part-time. When interpreting these figures, it is important to remember that this was a survey of nurses who were currently employed by the NHS. It seems likely that the effect of having children on the working patterns of female nurses would have been shown to be more marked if those who were no longer working as nurses had been included in the survey.

Part-time employment is now commonplace and a significant proportion of new job vacancies are offered on a part-time basis. Many employers, including the NHS, offer flexible working arrangements.[17] The vast majority of the flexible work-force are women. A major advantage of part-time employment is that it facilitates the combination of paid and unpaid work, particularly for women with children. But concern has been raised about the legal status of part-time employment and the quality of part-time jobs, which are often only available in 'low-level' employment and lead to few training or promotion opportunities (Plantenga, 1995). Indeed, we found few senior nurses working on a part-time basis (see Table 2.15). There may be an element of choice here, but it is also likely that part-time and flexible working conditions are not offered in these positions.

Household duties and the care of children and the elderly remain significant and time-consuming responsibilities for women. The lack of flexibility in working conditions and the lack of affordable and accessible childcare disadvantages women in employment. But there remains great potential for flexible employment strategies to offer a real solution to the conflict between home and work life. With such a high proportion of female nursing staff, the NHS could do much more to improve on the provision of flexible working arrangements and childcare facilities in all types of work and, importantly, for all grades of staff.

---

17. See Beishon *et al.* (1995: 109–123) for a qualitative examination of flexible working arrangements and childcare facilities in the NHS employers included in this survey.

Previous studies have found that childbirth is associated with downward occupational mobility, especially amongst women who return to part-time work (Dex, 1987; Waite *et al.*, 1989). Thus, both taking a career break to have children and working part-time have potential implications for the career progression of women, one of the issues we consider in the following chapter.

CHAPTER 5

Understanding Differences in the Career Progression of Male and Female Registered Nurses – Multivariate Analysis

INTRODUCTION

In earlier chapters we described a number of important differences between men and women in nursing. Women were: more likely to be enrolled nurses; more likely to work in particular specialities (such as the community and obstetrics and gynaecology); less likely to work in other specialities (such as mental illness or handicap); more likely to work part-time and nights; more likely to have taken a career break; less likely to expect to be encouraged to undertake further training; less likely to anticipate career progression; but equally likely to be career orientated. However, the key difference was that men were more likely to be in senior positions (see Table 2.2). How far this difference can be explained by the other gender differences outlined in previous chapters, or was the result of factors that the survey was unable to cover, will be the focus of this chapter, which is concerned with explaining why male registered nurses were more likely than female registered nurses to be in senior grades.

In order to tackle this, a multivariate approach to analysis was used, which essentially means considering more than one explanatory factor at a time. There are two reasons why such an approach is desirable. First, factors that might increase or decrease the chance of career progression for an individual may not act in isolation, each might act at the same time to either increase or decrease chances, or they might act in different directions. In addition, the relationships between particular explanatory factors do not occur by chance. If the explanatory factors under consideration are interrelated, when one factor is considered in isolation its true influence might be masked by its relationship to another that is not being considered. For example, we have already described that the older the respondent, the more likely it was that she or he would have taken a career break from nursing. However, age was positively related to career progression and taking breaks was negatively related to career progression. Unless both are considered together, the size of their influence on career progression would be underestimated. So without multivariate analysis it is impossible to separate out the effects of individual explanatory factors.

Second, earlier tables have shown that some of the explanatory factors to be considered vary by gender and, given that they were likely to make a significant impact on the chance of career progression, it would be worthwhile to see how far the gender difference in career progression for registered nurses remains once possible contributory factors are controlled for. However, as will be discussed later, the degree to which our measurement is accurate enough to provide an adequate degree of control over explanatory factors should be considered when interpreting the data presented.

Two techniques could be used for the multivariate analysis. One approach would be to consider the outcome – nursing grade – as a continuum with individual explanatory factors, including gender, acting similarly along the continuum. For example, it would seem logical to conclude that the more qualifications the respondent had, the more likely it would be that she or he would progress to more senior positions and that this effect would be similar for the transition from grades F to G, G to H and H to I. This would allow the use of techniques designed for the multivariate analysis of ordinal scales, such as ordered probit regression, to be used. In fact, this was the technique originally favoured for this analysis. However, as we progressed it became apparent that some of the key factors operated quite differently at different levels of the nursing hierarchy. An example of this, to be shown later (see Table 5.3), is that specialising in community nursing was positively related to the chances of obtaining a G grade, but negatively related to the chances of obtaining either a H or an I grade position. This made findings derived from this technique difficult to interpret and potentially misleading. Consequently, an alternative approach, logistic regression, has been adopted, where the analysis focuses on discrete outcomes and how various explanatory factors contribute to the chances of achieving these outcomes.

Two key outcomes are considered: being in a G grade position versus being in a lower grade; and being in a H or an I grade position versus being in a lower grade. Although there did not appear to be gender differences in the chances of being in a G grade position in Table 2.2, we have included this as one of our outcomes so that the analysis can focus on the range of grades among which a gender difference in outcome begins to emerge. This will allow the changing importance of particular factors on career progression to be identified as outcomes change. In addition, we have also considered independently the outcomes of being in a H grade position versus being in a lower grade and being in an I grade position versus being in a lower grade. This was so that differences between these two outcomes could be checked, although it should be recognised that this exploration is provisional as there were only a small number of respondents who were I grade.

As described earlier, the technique used to do this analysis was logistic regression, which allows an investigation of the chances of being in a particular nursing grade versus being in a lower grade. The data in the subsequent tables are laid out in terms of odds ratios for specific effects. These reflect the relative chance of an individual with a particular characteristic (such as being career orientated) achieving the outcome under consideration, compared with an individual with the reference characteristic (such as not being career orientated). The reference characteristics have an odds ratio of 1.0 in the tables. Odds ratios for the characteristics being compared with the reference that are greater than 1.0 indicate a greater chance of achieving the grade being considered, while those lower than 1.0 indicate a smaller chance. The further the odds ratio is from 1.0 (either higher or lower) the greater the effect. In addition to the size of an effect, we also need to consider the possibility that an effect has been found in these data as a result of chance. This has been done by identifying in the tables odds ratios that are statistically significant (ie not found by chance).

The influence of particular explanatory factors on gender differences in career progression can be seen by comparing the odds ratios for men compared with women in models with and without the explanatory factor. If the odds ratio for men compared to women decreases when the explanatory factor is included, it played some role in contributing to the gender difference. If the odds ratio increases, then taking account of the explanatory factor reveals that the difference between men and women was greater than it first appeared to be.

In order to increase the performance of the models presented, certain respondents have been excluded from them. First, it is important to remember that these models only concern registered nurses, because, as described in Box 1.1, enrolled and unqualified nurses cannot achieve promotion to the G, H and I grade positions under consideration. Second, those who were young or who had only recently qualified were extremely unlikely to be in more senior grades. Therefore, where G grade positions are considered, respondents who were younger than 25 or who had been registered for less than three years are excluded, and where H or I grade positions are considered, respondents who were younger than 30 or who had been registered for less than six years are excluded. Finally, in a survey such as this there are inevitably certain questions that individual respondents do not answer. In the subsequent models respondents are only included if they answered the questions concerning all of the factors under consideration. As the number of factors under consideration varies from model to model, the number of included respondents also varies.[18] This means that odds ratios for particular factors across models are not always identical.

Models will first be presented that separately show the effect of each explanatory factor once certain controls have been included. Once this has been done, a final set of models will be presented that show how taking account of all of the measured relevant factors affects the observed gender differences in career progression.

EXPLORING THE INFLUENCE OF PARTICULAR FACTORS ON CAREER POSITION

This section is concerned with assessing the contribution of particular factors to both nursing career progression and the influence of gender on that career progression. First, basic models containing gender and control factors are illustrated. Then models are shown illustrating the influence of particular explanatory factors once control factors have been included.

Base Models – Gender and Control Factors

Table 5.1 shows two basic models. The first contains only one explanatory variable – gender. As expected, it confirms the impression formed from Table 2.2: differences in the career progression of men and women in nursing did not emerge until they reached H grade. Men and women were equally likely to reach G grade, while men had twice the chance of reaching H or I grade. Differences in reaching H grade were smaller than this and not statistically significant, while differences in reaching I grade were much greater – men were more than four times more likely than women to be in an I grade post.

---

18. 13 per cent of the sample did not answer at least one of the questions used in the full model, shown in Table 5.7, so had to be excluded from it. The number of respondents excluded from the other models because of non-response to particular questionnaire items was smaller (because they included fewer questions), ranging from 7.5 per cent to 11 per cent of the sample.

Table 5.1 Models showing odds ratios for men compared to women with and without basic control factors

	G grade	H/I grade	H grade	I grade
Model 1: gender only				
Female	1.00	1.00	1.00	1.00
Male	0.93	2.04*	1.3	4.28*
Model 2: gender + human capital factors[1]				
Female	1.00	1.00	1.00	1.00
Male	1.54*	3.09*	1.97*	5.77*

*p < 0.01
1: These include: age, additional nursing qualifications held, years spent nursing and ethnic background. See text for a description of this.

Model 2 in Table 5.1 includes 'human capital' factors in addition to gender. The human capital factors included are those that, on the basis of Human Capital Theory (Becker, 1985), would be expected to be related to career progression and, consequently, they are regarded as basic controls. They are: age; additional nursing qualifications held; and years spent in nursing (excluding career breaks). All of these were related to career progression in the expected way – older respondents who had been nursing longer and who had more qualifications were more likely than others to be G, H or I grades. Among these basic controls we also included ethnic background. Ethnicity is not, of course, a human capital factor, but was included here because previous analysis of this data has shown it to be of importance in explaining career progression (for full details of the influence of ethnic background on career progression in nursing see Beishon *et al.*, 1995).

The comparison between the odds ratios for men in Model 2 and Model 1 is striking. Once the human capital factors had been taken into account, men were even more likely than women to reach senior positions – they were one and a half times more likely to be in grade G, compared with no difference without these control factors, and three times more likely to be in either grade H or I, compared to twice as likely without these control factors. If the odds for men compared with women of being in G, H and I grades are compared in Model 2, a picture of progressive advantage appears: this is illustrated in Figure 5.1. The odds go from 1.5 in the case of grade G, to 2 in the case of grade H, to almost 6 in the case of grade I. Taking into account statistical error, this suggests that once human capital factors had been taken into account men were between 3.8 and 8.7 times more likely than women to have reached grade I, between 1.3 and 2.9 times more likely to have reached grade H, and between 1.2 and 1.9 times more likely to have reached grade G.

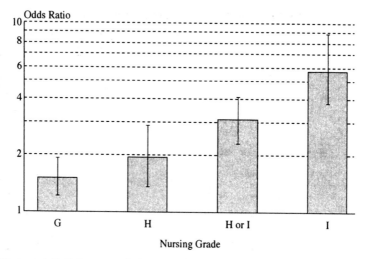

* Human capital includes: age, post-basic nursing qualifications, years spent working as a nurse, and ethnic background

Note: The odds ratios illustrated in Figure 5.1 reflect the relative chance of men being in a particular grade compared with women. So an odds ratio of 2 can be interpreted as 'twice as likely'. The further the odds ratio is from 1, the greater the effect. In the figures, the actual odds are represented by the solid bar. The lines are super-imposed on the bar to take account of statistical inaccuracies. They represent the range within which there is a 95 per cent probability that the true value of the odds ratio lies (95 per cent confidence limits). All differences shown are statistically significant.

Figure 5.1 Odds rations for men compared to women to be in particular nursing grades, adjusted for differences in human capital

Overall, the conclusions to be drawn from the comparisons of Models 1 and 2 are not reassuring. Model 1 shows the pattern of disadvantage that has been reported elsewhere for female nurses. Model 2 shows that if the explanatory factors that are not associated with gender-based discrimination[19] in the workplace are considered, the level of disadvantage is even greater. Here it is important to recognise the implication that standard comparisons between men and women in nursing that have not taken these factors into account will tend to underestimate the level of disadvantage faced by women.

Other Explanatory Factors

Table 5.2 shows odds ratios for one of the other explanatory factors that could be considered non- discriminatory – career orientation. Here the index of career orientation has been dichotomised into those who were and those who were not career orientated, based on whether the

19. The influence of ethnic background, which is included among these factors, on career progression is, of course, a consequence of anoth form of discrimination.

Table 5.2 Model showing odds ratios for career orientation

	G grade	H/I grade	H grade	I grade
Model 2 + career orientation				
Not career orientated	1.00	1.00	1.00	1.00
Career orientated	1.27**	1.53*	1.56*	1.37
Male	1.53*	3.12*	1.95*	6.12*

*p < 0.01
**p < 0.05

respondent had a score of three or more out of the items included (see Table 3.3). Table 5.2 shows clearly that career orientation was related to outcome – those who were more career orientated were more likely to be in grades G, H and I (although the difference for grade I was not statistically significant). The final row shows the odds ratios for men compared to women once career orientation, in addition to the human capital factors, had been taken into account. Comparing these with Model 2 (Table 5.1) shows that career orientation made no contribution to the differential career progression of men and women, despite its importance to an individual's progress. That is, the greater success of men compared to women in nursing could not be explained to any extent on the basis of differences in career orientation. In the light of the findings presented in Table 3.3, which illustrated the lack of difference in the career orientation of male and female nurses, this is, perhaps, not too surprising.

Table 5.3 explores the importance of the speciality worked in to career progression. Comparisons were made to working in medicine or surgery, which, consequently, have an odds ratio of one. Important differences were present between the different outcomes. For the G grade outcome, none of the specialities listed were less advantageous to career progression than medicine/surgery. Nurses working in both

Table 5.3 Model showing odds ratios for speciality worked in

	G grade	H/I grade	H grade	I grade
Model 2 + speciality				
Medicine/surgery	1.00	1.00	1.00	1.00
Obstetrics/gynaecology	2.83*	0.56*	0.42*	1.04
Paediatrics	1.16	0.93	0.80	1.34
Geriatrics	1.05	0.43*	0.26*	0.96
Mental illness/handicap	2.61*	1.15	1.05	1.48
Community	5.19*	0.58*	0.71**	0.27*
Male	1.58*	2.46*	1.70**	4.03*

*p < 0.01
**p < 0.05

Table 5.4 Model showing odds ratios for taking career breaks

	G grade	H/I grade	H grade	I grade
Model 2 + breaks from nursing				
No breaks taken	1.00	1.00	1.00	1.00
Taken a break for education	0.84	1.36	1.42	1.20
Taken a break for children, but < 1 year	0.70*	0.52*	0.56*	0.48*
Taken a break for children, 1 year plus	0.57*	0.37*	0.45*	0.24*
Taken a break for another reason	1.03	0.71**	0.84	0.50*
Male	1.19	2.01*	1.34	3.40*

*p < 0.01
**p < 0.05

obstetrics/gynaecology and mental illness/handicap had more than a two-fold greater likelihood of reaching a G grade position, and nurses working in the community had a five-fold greater likelihood of reaching this position, than those working in the reference speciality (medicine or surgery).

In contrast, those working in the community had a smaller chance of being in either a H or an I grade position and, for the latter outcome, the chances were very small compared to those working in medicine/surgery. In fact, although differences were smaller for the other specialities, respondents working in all of them were less likely to be in H or I grade positions than respondents working in medicine/surgery, except those working in mental illness/handicap who had a slightly higher, but not statistically significantly greater, chance.

The importance of this structural difference in career paths for gender differences in career progression can be seen from Table 2.3, which illustrates that women and men were likely to work in different specialities. In particular, men were more likely to work in mental illness/handicap and women were more likely to work in obstetrics/gynaecology and the community. The final row of Table 5.3 shows the odds ratios for men compared with women to reach particular grades once the human capital factors and speciality had been taken into account. Differences remained large and statistically significant. However, comparing the figures with those shown in Table 5.1 for Model 2 shows that, while the odds were not reduced for G grades, they were for H and I grades. This suggests that part of the explanation for gender differences in career progression lies in the different specialities that men and women work in.

The next three tables focus on issues relating to family-friendly working patterns. That is, the extent to which career progression, and gender differences in this, were a consequence of: taking career breaks; working particular shift patterns; and working part-time. Table 5.4 shows the influence of taking breaks on career progression. Odds ratios are shown in relation to those who had not taken a break. For those who had taken a break for education, once again there was a contradictory pattern according to outcome – chances were increased for reaching H or I grade posts, but decreased for reaching a G grade post. However, none of these differences were statistically significant so should be interpreted with caution.

Respondents who had taken a career break for having children were less likely than those who had not taken a break to reach any of the outcomes shown. In addition, their chances decreased with the length of the break taken and with the seniority of the post considered. It is important here to recollect that this effect is in addition to the decreased amount of time they had spent working, which was accounted for by one of the human capital factors that was also present in the model (years spent in nursing). Taking a career break for other reasons also decreased the likelihood of reaching a H or I grade position, but not by as much and it made no difference to the chances of reaching a G grade position. The final row shows the odds ratios for men compared with women to reach particular grades once the effect of taking career breaks had been taken into account. Comparing these odds ratios with those shown for Model 2 in Table 5.1 suggests that taking breaks made an important contribution to gender differences in career progression. In each case the odds ratios were substantially reduced (for example, men's greater chances of being in an I grade position fell from about 5.8 to 3.4) and they became no longer statistically significant for G and H grade positions.

Table 5.5 shows how the chances of reaching particular grades varied according to the shift pattern worked by registered nurses, again once the human capital factors had been taken into account. The comparison is made to those nurses who worked days only (ie only

Table 5.5 Model showing odds ratios for shift patterns worked

	G grade	H/I grade	H grade	I grade
Model 2 + shift patterns worked				
Days or earlies only	1.00	1.00	1.00	1.00
Rotating	0.33*	0.26*	0.26*	0.28*
Nights only	0.10*	0.06*	0.09*	< 0.01
Male	1.43*	3.05*	2.05*	5.49*

*p < 0.01

Table 5.6 Model showing odds ratios for hours worked

	G grade	H/I grade	H grade	I grade
Model 2 + hours worked				
35 or more	1.00	1.00	1.00	1.00
24 to 34	0.45*	0.25*	0.29*	0.17*
Less than 24	0.39*	0.12*	0.16*	0.01*
Male	1.12	2.03*	1.34	3.60*

*p < 0.01

9am to 5pm or earlies), who consequently have an odds ratio of 1.0. Nurses who worked rotating shifts were much less likely to be in any of the more senior grades, while those who worked nights only were unlikely to be in G grade positions and extremely unlikely to be in H or I grade positions. The final row shows the odds ratios for men compared to women once the shift patterns worked had been taken into account. Comparing this with those in Model 2 shows that there was very little difference, which means that although women were more likely than men to be working nights (see Table 2.4) this made no difference to gender differences in career progression.

The final model in this section takes account of full- and part-time working, and is shown in Table 5.6. Comparisons are made to those who worked at least 35 hours a week. The odds ratios for part-time workers show that they were significantly less likely than full-time workers to be in any of these grades. In addition, these differences increased with seniority and with decreasing number of hours worked. Nurses who worked fewer than 24 hours a week were very unlikely to have been in a H grade post and had almost no chance of being in a I grade post. Table 2.5 shows that female nurses were much more likely than male nurses to be working part-time – almost a quarter of female registered nurses worked less than 24 hours a week compared to only 2 per cent of male registered nurses. A comparison between the final row of Table 5.6 and Model 2 in Table 5.1 shows how much of a contribution this made to gender differences in career progression. Once hours worked had been taken into account, there were minimal gender differences in the chances of being in a G grade post and the gender differences in the chances of being in a H or an I grade post were much reduced, although still large and still statistically significant.

Summary

This exploration of the influences of particular factors on career progression in nursing and how these affected gender differences allows us to reach some preliminary conclusions. One possible explanation for differences in career progression is that they were a result of differences in the experience, level of qualifications and other human capital factors between men and women. However, comparisons between Model 1 and Model 2 shown in Table 5.1 illustrate that the opposite was the case. Once such human capital factors had been taken into account, the extent of women's disadvantage became even more apparent.

An alternative explanation is that gender differences in career progression were the result of men's greater orientation towards a career. Table 3.3 suggested that women were just as orientated as men towards a career in nursing. And a comparison between Table 5.2 and Table 5.1 shows that although career orientation was related to career success, taking account of it did not alter gender differences.

The tables in Chapter 2 also showed gender differences in patterns of working. Men and women were more likely to work in different specialities, women were more likely to have taken career breaks, to work nights and to work part-time. Tables 5.3 to 5.6 showed that all of these factors were related to career progression and that all, apart from shift patterns worked, had some influence on gender differences. The implications of this will be discussed more fully in the conclusion to this chapter. However, before this is done there is a need to explore the degree to which the combined effects of the factors so far considered influence gender differences in career progression. Interrelationships between explanatory factors may lead to cumulative effects reducing gender differences even further, or they may cancel each other out. This will be the focus of the next section.

EXPLAINING GENDER DIFFERENCES

In order to assess the degree to which the factors included in previous models contributed to gender differences in career progression when jointly considered, logistic regression was once again used. As before outcomes were split into being in: grade G versus a lower grade; grade H and I versus a lower grade; grade H versus a lower grade; and grade I versus a lower grade. This allowed us to take into account the possibility that different factors were of more or less importance for gender differences at various career points. The logistic regression models were built using a stepwise approach. This allowed comparisons to be made between the odds ratios for men compared with women of being in particular grades as additional explanatory factors were entered into the model. The findings of this process are shown in Table 5.7 and are illustrated in Figure 5.2 for the H/I grade outcome.

Table 5.7 The importance of various explanatory factors on gender differences in career progression

	G grade	H/I grade	H grade	I grade
			odds ratios for men compared to women	
Factors added to the model				
i. gender only	0.83	2.10*	1.44[as]	4.12*
ii. + human capital factors[1]	1.39*	3.31*	2.27*	5.68*
iii. + career orientation	1.37*	3.28*	2.25*	5.68*
iv. + speciality	1.42*	2.49*	1.85*	3.67*
v. + shifts worked	1.35	2.41*	1.83**	3.48*
vi. + hours worked	1.09	1.94*	1.50	2.78*
vii. + breaks taken (excluding education)	0.99	1.63**	1.28	2.30*
viii. + breaks for education	1.00	1.63**	1.28	2.29*

*p < 0.01
**p < 0.05
[as]p< 0.06
1: These include: age, additional nursing qualifications held, years spent nursing and ethnic background.

They confirm the impressions formed from earlier tables. The first set of factors added were those relating to human capital and including these in the model increased gender differences in career progression – men became much more likely than women to reach all of these grades. Next, career orientation was entered into the model and, as would be expected on the basis of previous tables and models, this did not alter gender differences for any of the outcomes. After this, speciality worked in was added. This made no difference to the G grade outcome, but decreased gender differences for the H and I grade outcomes, although they remained large and statistically significant. The order of the next three factors added into the model – shifts worked, hours worked and breaks taken (excluding those for education) – was based on the strength of their contribution to reaching the grade under consideration. Table 5.7 shows that for all outcomes, as each new factor was added gender differences in career progression decreased, although the influence of shifts worked was small. The overall size of the decrease was large – the odds ratios for men compared with women had more than halved from their highs at points ii and iii by the time point vii was reached. For the H or I grade outcome the odds ratio had fallen from about 3.3 to 1.6, but the difference was still statistically significant (see Figure 5.2). For the G grade outcome, taking account of these factors left the model with no gender difference (the odds ratio had fallen from about 1.4 to 1.0). The final

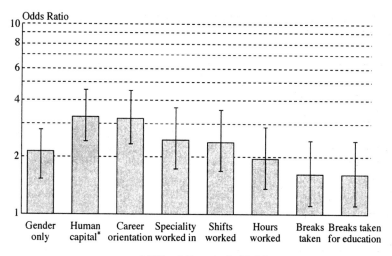

Additional Factor in the Model

* Human capital includes: age, post-basic nursing qualifications, years spent working as a nurse, and ethnic background

Note: The odds ratios illustrated in Figure 5.2 reflect the relative chance of men being in a particular grade compared with women. So an odds ratio of 2 can be interpreted as 'twice as likely'. The further the odds ratio is from 1, the greater the effect. In the figures, the actual odds are represented by the solid bar. The lines are super-imposed on the bar to take account of statistical inaccuracies. They represent the range within which there is a 95 per cent probability that the true value of the odds ratio lies (95 per cent confidence limits). All differences shown are statistically significant.

Figure 5.2 Changes in odds ratios for men compared to women to be in H or I grade positions when explanatory factors are taken into account

factor included in the model was taking breaks for education and this made no contribution to gender differences for any of the outcomes. Thus, once these factors had been taken into account the following became evident:

- Men were no more likely than women to be in G grade positions (their odds ratio had fallen from a high of 1.4 to 1.0).
- Men were still more likely to be in either a H or an I grade position, but the odds ratio had fallen from a high of 3.3 to 1.6.
- However, considering H grades on their own suggests that men were not more likely to be in these positions (their odds ratio had fallen from a high of 2.3 to 1.3, a difference that was not statistically significant).
- While considering I grades separately suggests that men were over twice as likely to be in this grade, although the odds ratio had fallen from a high of 5.7 to 2.3.

It is worth also noting that if marital status is considered in these models, married or cohabiting men appeared to be significantly advantaged compared to both their single counterparts and women (although small sample sizes made this difficult to examine in full). Considering the H or I grade outcome, while marital status made little difference to the chances of women being in this position, it made an important difference for men. Single men had the same chance as women while the odds ratio for married or cohabiting men compared with women was about 1.8, a statistically significant difference. This 'marriage premium' is inconsistent with the interpretation of traditional human capital theory that has guided much of this analysis, but it is consistent with a household production model. Here it is recognised that two can live more easily than one resulting in an individual becoming more productive once married. It is also consistent with a selection model, in which doing well in the labour market is correlated with doing well in the 'marriage market' (Waldfogel, 1997). However, in both the household production and the selection models the advantage applies to men, not women.

DISCUSSION

The logistic regression models shown in Tables 5.1 to 5.7 showed how gender differences in career progression varied as three sets of explanatory factors were considered. These were: differences in human capital, such as additional nursing qualifications held; differences in career orientation; and structural differences in opportunities. The first two of these explanations are not related to direct gender-based discrimination.[20] The third is not necessarily a consequence of discrimination, but can certainly be considered as adversely affecting the careers of women to an unjustifiable extent.

Once gender differences in human capital had been taken into account, women were found to be even more at a disadvantage compared with men across all of the outcomes under consideration. In addition, the level of disadvantage increased as the seniority of the post increased. Career orientation was found to be related to career progression, but, because women were just as likely as men to be career orientated, this factor did not explain any of the disadvantage faced by women in career progression.

However, the structural factors under consideration appeared to make a significant contribution to the disadvantage faced by women.

---

20. Though women may accumulate less human capital, or be less career-orientated due to anticipated disadvantage, otherwise known as pre-market discrimination (Elliott, 1991)

Of those considered, shift patterns worked appeared to make the least contribution and perhaps can be disregarded as an important part of gender differences (although, like career orientation, it was important when considering an individual's chances of career progression). The other three factors, speciality worked in, taking career breaks (mainly in order to have or care for children) and working part-time all made an important contribution to women's disadvantage in career progression in nursing. Once these had been taken into account, men's greater chances of success had been substantially reduced for all of the outcomes. However, men were still about two-thirds more likely to be in a H or I grade position (compared with being over three times more likely when these factors were not taken into account) and this difference remained statistically significant. This means that women who worked full-time, who did not work in 'female' specialities (such as obstetrics, gynaecology and in the community) and who had not taken career breaks were only slightly disadvantaged compared with men (although some of the differences were still statistically significant), while women to whom one or more of these things applied were substantially disadvantaged compared with men.

It seems likely that the difference that remained between men and women in the models once various explanatory factors had been considered was a consequence of one of three possibilities. First, it is possible that it was a consequence of inaccuracies in the measurement of factors included in the models. These inaccuracies are inevitable and will be at their largest in a postal, self-completion survey such as this. At one level such inaccuracies result from misunderstandings and mistakes made by respondents when filling in the questionnaires, at another they will result from the crude categories that are used to measure particular factors – such as the simple distinction between certificates, diplomas and degrees when considering additional nursing qualifications held. Both of these forms of inaccuracy will reduce the precision with which explanatory factors are measured and consequently reduce their assessed influence on the outcome under consideration.

Second, it is possible that the remaining differences between men and women were a consequence of excluding some dimensions of the explanatory factors that were included. This is particularly a problem for a cross-sectional survey such as this which attempts to explain a current position with current assessments of explanatory factors. For example, career orientation was based on a measure of current perceptions of reasons for initially entering nursing. No matter how accurate those perceptions were, the degree of career orientation may have changed over time and such changes may have led to differences in outcome. Similarly, assessments of part-time working were based on the current post. Some of those respondents who currently worked full-time might have worked part-time in the past, and this may have influenced their career progression.

Both of these possibilities suggest that the models would have explained more of the gender difference in career progression if our measurement had been more accurate. Whether it would have altered the balance among the three explanatory items included is less clear. However, it could be suggested that if the pattern followed that already established, a more accurate assessment of human capital factors would have further increased gender differences, a more accurate assessment of career orientation would have continued to make no difference, and a more accurate assessment of structural factors would have decreased gender differences in career progression even further.

The third possibility is that the remaining gender difference in career progression was a consequence of a factor that was not included in any of the models. Most likely here is that it was a result of direct gender-based discrimination. This will be discussed further below, but it does seem likely that direct discrimination does play a role, although given the degree of difference remaining, it may be of less importance to career progression than the explanatory factors that were directly considered.

Overall, then, the models suggest that structural factors played the key role in disadvantaging women compared with men in nursing. However, where the significance of the structural factors lies appears to vary. In terms of hours worked, part-time work could be seen to reduce the chances of promotion to more senior positions in two ways. First, those who work part-time could be looked on less favourably when promotion is considered and this could occur for a number of reasons. Second, those who prefer to work part-time may find that there are very few part-time jobs in more senior positions and, consequently, they may not have the opportunity to both continue working part-time and apply for more senior jobs. The latter possibility certainly seems to be at least part of the explanation here. Table 2.17 showed that there were very few respondents in senior positions who worked part-time. Given the importance of part-time work for women with families, the lack of opportunities to work part-time in more senior positions must be considered a problem.

The findings for speciality worked in are likely to be a reflection of two possible factors – the opportunities for promotion within particular specialities and the level of competition for the posts that are available. The data suggest that, unlike for part-time work, the issue was not simply a lack of senior jobs in particular specialities. Indeed, of the registered nurses working in the community, 10 per cent were in the senior H or I grade posts. Among those working in mental illness/handicap a similar proportion were in H or I grade posts, but for all of the other specialities the figure was 6 per cent or lower. Consequently, the issue might have been one of relative competition for the posts that were available. Indeed, almost 60 per cent of registered nurses working in the community were in G grade posts, giving a ratio of G to H or I grade posts of 5.6 to one. Ratios of G to H or I grade posts for medicine/surgery, paediatrics, and mental illness/handicap were all in the region of three to one. The ratio for geriatrics was similar to that for the community, while that for obstetrics/gynaecology was almost nine to one. These ratios suggest that in particular specialities – the community, obstetrics/gynaecology and geriatrics – there is greater competition for jobs above G grade, and, apart from geriatrics where equal proportions of men and women work, these are the specialities where women are more likely than men to work.

Of course the models presented here give no indication as to why men and women were more likely to be found in different specialities. Respondents were not asked why they worked in particular areas so we can say little about this. However, three factors may be important. First, men and women may choose to work in different specialities, for example men may be less likely to want to work in obstetrics, perhaps because they see themselves as having a comparative disadvantage in this speciality. Second, certain specialities may offer fewer obstacles for family-friendly patterns of work, for example community-based work might be more flexible than hospital-based work. Third, the differences might be a result of discrimination, for example employers may feel that men are more capable of dealing with the security-related problems that may be present for those looking after the mentally ill.

The interpretation of the finding for taking career breaks is less clear than for the other factors. It seems that this may be a consequence of a deterioration in (perceived) human capital once the break has been taken. Nurses who take such career breaks may be viewed as having lost their skills and may, as others have suggested, have to return to more junior posts than those that they had had prior to taking their break (Waite *et al.*, 1989). The extent to which this, and a possible subsequent slowing of career progression, was a consequence of direct discrimination against those who have taken breaks is open to question.

CHAPTER 6

Conclusion

This report presents results from a detailed analysis exploring the influence of gender on the career paths of nurses. The analysis was based on a postal survey of 14,330 nursing and midwifery staff working in the NHS in 1994. The survey covered both unqualified and qualified staff, nurses in grades A to I, and nurses working in a variety of specialities. Differences in the occupational profiles and attitudes and expectations of male and female nursing staff were described. An issue central to any investigation of gender differences in employment – women's greater household and family responsibilities – was explored in detail. Finally, multivariate analysis testing key explanations for men's greater likelihood to be found in more senior positions was conducted.

The strengths of this survey for exploring the issues relevant to gender differences in nursing have been discussed. Important here is the size of the survey – the largest survey of nurses ever undertaken – which meant that sufficient male nurses were included for a detailed analysis of gender differences. Also important was that the sampling strategy adopted and a fairly high response rate to the questionnaire means that we can be reasonably confident that the findings are representative of the nursing work-force that was employed in the NHS in 1994. However, the study has one important disadvantage: it was a study of those who were directly employed by the NHS, which meant that nurses who had given up nursing work, or who worked part-time through nursing agencies, were not included in the study. One of the key differences between men and women may be that, because of their domestic responsibilities, women are more likely than men to give up nursing completely, or to only do bank nursing. If either of these were the case, our reliance on a sample that was currently employed in the NHS would lead to an underestimation of gender differences in career progression. The importance of this will be returned to later.

KEY FINDINGS

The following provides an overview of the findings shown in earlier chapters of this volume.

The Position of Men and Women in Nursing

- Men made up 7.2 per cent of the sample overall.
- Men were less likely than women to be in unqualified nursing positions and much less likely to be enrolled nurses.
- Men were more likely to be found in higher grades for all three types of nurse. For registered nurses, differences appeared to emerge above G grade – men were twice as likely as women to be in either a H or an I grade position.
- There were differences in the types of specialities that men and women worked in. Women were more likely to work in obstetrics or gynaecology, paediatrics, or in the community, and men were more likely to work in mental illness/handicap. Senior female registered nurses were more likely to be working in the community than their junior counterparts.
- About 45 per cent of women worked part-time (less than 35 hours per week) compared with just over 5 per cent of men. Part-time working was less common among registered nurses. Senior female registered nurses were considerably less likely to be working part-time than their junior counterparts, but still more likely to do so than men.
- Women were more likely than men to be working nights only, while men were more likely to be working a rotating shift pattern.
- Registered and unqualified female nurses had been in nursing longer than their male equivalents.
- Qualified female nurses felt more restricted than qualified male nurses in their ability to take paid time off work, to go on training courses and in getting their course fees paid.
- A greater proportion of unqualified male nursing staff than equivalent females had been encouraged to take further training. They also said that they would find it easier to get their course fees paid.
- Men were more likely than women to have post A-level non-nursing qualifications, but less likely to have obtained additional post-basic nursing qualifications. Senior female nurses were considerably better qualified than their male counterparts.

Perceptions, Attitudes and Expectations of Nurses

- Having rewarding, interesting and a variety of work were the reasons most likely to have been very important for all nursing staff in entering the nursing profession.
- Women were more orientated than men towards non-instrumental rewards, such as having rewarding and interesting work, whereas men were more orientated than women towards instrumental rewards, in particular pay and the prospect of promotion.
- However, there was no significant difference between male and female nursing staff in overall orientation towards having a career.
- Rates of overall satisfaction with their jobs were very low among nursing staff when compared with findings from general population surveys.
- Men were less satisfied with their work and grade than women.
- Men were more likely than women to expect to move to a better job (higher grade or preferred speciality) in the near future. One in six women were expecting to be raising a family in the near future.

Family Responsibilities and Barriers to Work

- A fifth of the sample had pre-school children and a further fifth had dependent children aged six to fifteen.
- Women were considerably more likely than men to have taken a career break and were also more likely to have taken a longer break. Women were ten times more likely than men to have taken a career break in order to care for children.
- For women, being married or cohabiting increased their chances of working part-time, regardless of the presence of children.
- Having dependent children also increased the chances of working part-time for women.
- Of the family-friendly shifts available to nurses, on the whole only those that involved part-time work or nights only work were more frequently used by women with children than men.
- Parents felt that the childcare facilities offered by their employers were unsatisfactory.

Understanding Gender Differences in Career Progression

- A number of factors beyond gender were shown to be related to career progression in nursing. These included: human capital factors, such as level of education and experience; career orientation; speciality worked in; taking career breaks; working particular shifts; and working part-time.
- Once human capital factors had been taken into account, the extent of women's disadvantage in career progression, compared with men, became even more apparent.
- Although career orientation was related to career success, taking account of this did not alter gender differences in career progression.
- When considered on their own, speciality worked in, shift patterns and hours worked, and career breaks all appeared to make a significant contribution to the disadvantage in career progression that was faced by women.
- When all of the possible explanatory factors were considered together, structural factors relating to part-time working and taking career breaks to have children appeared to play a key role in disadvantaging women compared with men in nursing.
- Once all potential explanatory factors had been taken into account, the odds ratio for men to be in a G grade position compared with women dropped from 1.4 to 1.0, while to be in a H or an I grade position they dropped for 3.3 to 1.6.
- So, the multivariate analysis showed that, after taking account of such factors, a gender difference in the chances of reaching the more senior positions remained and was statistically significant, though it was greatly reduced. Remaining gender differences could be the result of the imprecision of the models built for this analysis, or a result of the influence of factors that were not directly measured in this survey, such as direct discrimination against women.

Explaining Men's Career Advantage in Nursing

The findings presented in this volume show quite clearly that men do better than women in their nursing careers. This difference was present for unqualified, enrolled and registered nurses, although it was only examined in detail for registered nurses. It seems that their are four possible reasons for this gender difference. First, men may be better qualified to do the work, that is, they may have a higher average human capital (Becker, 1985; Mincer and Polachek, 1974). However, when we explored the influence of human capital on the differences found here, we found that taking account of them made men's advantage even more apparent. They seemed to be doing better than women despite being less experienced and having poorer post-basic nursing qualifications.

Second, the differences may be a consequence of men having a greater orientation to a career and work, perhaps as a result of some women's greater orientation to the home (Hakim, 1995). We were only able to use a surrogate indicator for career orientation (based on the reasons given by respondents for entering nursing), but this indicator was found to be related to career progression. However, it did not show any differences in the career orientation of women compared with men and did not explain any of the career advantage that men had.

Third, the differences might have resulted from organisational barriers to career progression that resulted in disadvantage for women. We assessed a number of dimensions of this and found that three in particular contributed a great deal to men's career advantage – differences between the specialities that men and women worked in and their consequent opportunities for advancement; women's greater likelihood to work part-time; and women's greater likelihood to have taken a career break in order to have children. The ways in which these factors may have differentially influenced the chances of career progression for men and women is, however, complex. At one level it seems that the jobs that were most family-friendly, i.e. that were the most convenient for women who also had family responsibilities, were those that were the least likely to be senior. It is certainly the case that there were very few part-time senior jobs. At another level, it seems that the senior jobs to which women had the greatest access were also those for which there was also the greatest competition, as seemed to be the case for those who were working in obstetrics and gynaecology and in the community. It is also likely that some of this disadvantage was linked to the extent to which some of the family-friendly options, which were taken for the most part by women, did not meet the organisational 'norms' within nursing and, consequently, resulted in the perception that women taking these options were less suitable promotion material. This may well have applied to those that took career breaks to have a family – the disadvantage of such women could not be explained on the basis of their qualifications, their experience, nor their reported initial orientation to a career. And it must be remembered that this effect was in addition to the actual time taken out of paid employment by taking a career break, which was already taken into account in the models (years spent in nursing). This explanation may also have applied to those that worked part-time.

Finally, the differences may have been a result of direct discrimination faced by women. In this survey no attempt has been made to assess the extent of direct discrimination faced by women. Rather, we have partly followed the tradition of empirical work conducted using a human capital framework (Becker, 1964; Mincer and Polachek, 1974), where the gap that remains after other explanatory factors have been taken into account can be attributed to gender-based discrimination. Applying this tradition strictly suggests that such discrimination plays an important role – men had an odds ratio compared with women of 1.6 to be in a H or an I grade position once key factors had been taken into account and if I grade positions are considered on their own, the odds ratio was an even greater 2.4. There was some supporting, if indirect, evidence for the suggestion that gender-based discrimination might be occurring. For example, although women were just as likely as men to be career orientated, they were less likely to believe that they would be promoted in the near future. Women were also less likely than men to believe that they would be supported if they wanted to undertake post-basic training. However, we feel that the remaining gap should be interpreted more cautiously. As discussed in the conclusion to Chapter 5, at least part of the remaining difference could have been a result of inaccuracies in the models developed, which may have led to the importance of organisational barriers being underestimated.

Overall then, of the four explanations considered we can conclude that there were minimal differences in the initial career orientation of men and women and that these played no role in men's career advantage over women. Taking account of differences in human capital in fact made gender differences in career progression even more apparent. Organisational barriers played a large and important role in the disadvantage faced by women. Evidence also existed for direct discrimination against women, but, because we had no direct assessment of this, we cannot be confident of its extent nor the degree of influence it exerted.

Finally, we must return to the problems of having conducted this survey only among nurses who were currently employed by the NHS. Because of this, the women in this sample may represent a select group of 'survivors' who had, to a certain extent at least, coped with the barriers that they faced in order to continue in paid work. This may mean that the women facing the greatest disadvantages were not represented in our sample, as they had the greatest chance of being absent from the labour market altogether. This would mean that we have greatly underplayed the impact of organisational barriers on the poorer career success of women. On the other hand, our sample may include women with a greater career orientation or who were less 'home-centred'. This would mean that we have underestimated the importance of career orientation to gender differences in career success (but not that we have overestimated the importance of organisational barriers). Either way, we have been able to show the differences between *working* men and women in the NHS and at least part of the reason for men's greater career success.

IMPLICATIONS

Men and women were likely to be working in different specialities and women were more likely than men to have taken a career break(s), to work nights and to work part-time. All these factors related to career progression and all, except shift patterns worked, had some influence on the gender difference in the career paths of nurses. As described above, we found that these organisational barriers played the key role in disadvantaging women compared with men in nursing. Although not directly discriminatory,[21] the structures within organisations that penalise part-time work and breaks from employment *adversely impact to an unjustifiable extent* the careers of those who are unable, or unwilling, to work full-time hours, or who have had interrupted employment. These factors particularly apply to women with children.

The increasing flexibility of the labour market has the potential to benefit all parties – for employers, flexibility brings cost and efficiency gains and for employees, flexible forms of work enable the combination of work and family duties (Casey *et al.*, 1997). However, this increased flexibility should not come at a cost to the (predominantly female) flexible workforce: part-time work often attracts poor conditions of employment and limited opportunities for promotion and career development (Callender, 1996; Plantenga, 1995). Employers in general should be committed to providing flexibility of employment and to improving the conditions of flexible work. Only by doing so can we move towards greater equality of opportunity for women in the labour market. Such a strategy would enable employers to make more use of the qualifications, experience and commitment of their female staff (Metcalf, 1997). This would also increase the recruitment and retention rates among those with family and caring responsibilities at home. Otherwise it is likely that employers, including the NHS, will continue to lose out by leaving female staff in posts that do not allow them to use their skills to their full and to develop these skills.

The NHS, consequently, should re-evaluate its commitment to part-time and flexible contracts. It should provide part-time working arrangements in all specialities and, in particular, for all grades of staff

---

21. The previous section describes how direct discrimination may have played a role as well.

including more senior positions. It should carefully examine how to promote the careers of women who have taken career breaks and who may, subsequently, wish to engage in part-time work. And it should examine how the experience of particular groups of nurses is neither rewarded nor benefited from, because they work in specialities that restrict their opportunities for promotion. Finally, we have said little about childcare, but the finding that most parents felt that the child-care facilities made available to them by their employers were bad and more than two out of five felt that they were very bad, suggests that this is one of the most important areas for reform, both within the NHS and also more generally.

Of course, the position of women within the NHS is already a central concern for many. Both the Department of Health and the NHS Management Executive have commissioned a number of reports on relevant issues (for example: Chiplin with Greig, 1986; Davies and Rosser, 1986; Goss and Brown, 1991; Davies with Conn, 1993), including the work presented here. There appears to be general agreement that 'The National Health Service is the largest employer of women in Western Europe, but its employment policies and practices are far from being woman-friendly' (Equal Opportunities Commission, 1991: 3). Following these reports, several strategies to address the small proportion of women in senior positions have been suggested and adopted. Much of this has focused on two themes. The strongest theme that has emerged is the need for clearly stated equal opportunities policies throughout the NHS and a firm commitment to them. For example, of the 13 recommendations made to Districts, Units and Trusts by the Equal Opportunities Commission report (1991), nine involved equal opportunities policies, and two involved a monitoring of possible discrimination. However, within the NHS there is evidence to suggest that progress on equal opportunities has been very uneven (NHS Equal Opportunities Unit, 1997). The suggestion in the data presented here, that discrimination may play an important role in producing gender differences illustrates the importance of more effective monitoring of equality outcomes.

The second theme that has emerged is the need for the counselling and mentoring of individuals towards senior positions, in order to help them through the 'glass ceiling'. However, the data in this report suggest that the problem is more fundamental and requires more far-reaching organisational changes. The 'glass ceiling' is almost certainly a misnomer. Difficulties for women are present at relatively junior positions, for example in the transition from F to G grade, and they become greater as seniority increases. It is more like wading through setting cement – progress starts of easily but becomes increasingly more difficult as the cement begins to set (begins to move up grades) then comes to a complete standstill as the cement sets completely (hit the glass ceiling). The source of such difficulties appears to be largely located in the organisational barriers described above. The most effective way to improve the situation is for employers to carefully consider how the organisational barriers faced by women undertaking paid work can be reduced. And this has important implications for both NHS and non-NHS employers.

Although there has been a fair amount of discussion on flexible work in the reports cited above, this is the area that has received the least emphasis. The evidence presented here suggests it should receive the most. In order to address gender differences in career progression, four crucial factors must be addressed: the unduly negative impact of career breaks on the chances of career progression; the lack of opportunities for part-time work in senior posts; the lack of opportunities for promotion from the specialities within which women are more likely to be located; and the great inadequacy of the childcare provision by both NHS employers and others. Recent equality objectives set out in the NHS White Paper (DoH, 1997), including the development of family-friendly and flexible employment practices are therefore crucial in order to address men's career advantage in nursing.

Finally, the very high levels of dissatisfaction with their work reported by both male and female respondents to this survey compared with those reported by the general population (Clark, 1996) must be a cause for great concern. The recruitment and retention of nurses is a key issue facing the NHS (Price Waterhouse, 1998) and there is a clear link between overall job satisfaction and staying in a job, which may be stronger for women (Clark, 1996). Thus, the dimensions underlying the dissatisfaction nurses have with their work warrants further investigation and detailed consideration of how they might be addressed.

References

Becker, G. (1957) *The Economics of Discrimination*, Chicago: University of Chicago Press

Becker, G. (1964) *Human Capital*, New York: Columbia University Press

Becker, G. (1985) 'Human Capital, Effort and the Sexual Division of Labour', *Journal of Labour Economics*, vol. 3, pp. 33–38

Beishon, S., Virdee, S. & Hagell, A. (1995) *Nursing in a Multi-Ethnic NHS*, London: Policy Studies Institute

Berndt, E. R. (1991) *The Practice of Econometrics: Classic and Contemporary*, Reading: Addison-Wesley

Buchan, J. & Seccombe, I. (1991) *Nurses' Work and Worth, IMS Report No. 213*, Brighton: Institute of Manpower Studies

Buchan, J., Waite, R. & Thomas, J. (1989) *Grade Expectations: Clinical Grading and Nurse Mobility, IMS Report No.176*, Brighton: Institute of Manpower Studies

Caines, K. & Hammond, V. (1996) *Creative Career Paths in the NHS: The Agenda for Action*, London: Department of Health

Callender, C. (1996) 'Women and Employment' in C. Hallett (ed.), *Women and Social Policy*, Hemel Hempstead: Harvester Wheatsheaf

Casey, B., Metcalf, H. & Millward, N. (1997) *Employers' Use of Flexible Labour*, London: Policy Studies Institute

Chiplin, B with Greig, N. (1986) *Equality of Opportunity for Women in the NHS*, London: Department of Health and Social Security

Clark, A. E. (1996) 'Job Satisfaction in Britain', *British Journal of Industrial Relations*, vol. 34, no. 2, pp. 189–217

Davidson, M. J. and Cooper, C. L. (1992) *Shattering the Glass Ceiling: The Woman Manager*, London: Paul Chapman Publishing Ltd

Davies, C. with Conn, L. (1993) *Creating Compatible Careers*, London: Department of Health

Davies, C. & Rosser, J. (1984) *A Report on a Survey of Senior Nurses in Central District*, Coventry: University of Warwick (unpublished report)

Davies, C. & Rosser, J. (1986) *Processes of discrimination: A study of women working in the NHS*, London: Department of Health and Social Security

Department of Health (1995) *NHS Workforce in England 1982–1992*, London: HMSO

Department of Health (1997) *The New NHS – modern, dependable*, London: The Stationery Office

Dex, J. (1987) *Women's Occupational Mobility: a Lifetime Perspective*, London: Macmillan

Elliot, R. F. (1991) *Labor Economics: A Comparative Text*, London: McGraw-Hill

Equal Opportunities Commission (1991) *Equality Management. Women's Employment in the NHS*, Manchester: Equal Opportunities Commission

Finlayson, L., Ford, R. & Marsh, A. (1996) 'Paying More for Childcare', *Labour Market Trends*, July, pp. 295–303

Ford, R. (1996) *Childcare in the Balance*, London: Policy Studies Institute

The Financial Times 'Women Managers Fare Badly', 28th January 1997

Gaze, H. (1987) 'Men in Nursing', *Nursing Times*, vol. 83, no. 20, pp. 25–27

Ginn, J. , Arber, S., Brannen, J., Dale, A., Dex, S., Elias, P., Moss, P., Pahl, J., Roberts, C. & Rubery, J. (1996) 'Feminist Fallacies: a Reply to Hakim on Women's Employment', *British Journal of Sociology*, vol. 47, no. 1, pp. 167–174

Goss, S. & Brown, H. (1991) *Equal Opportunities for Women in the NHS*, London: NHS Management Executive

Hakim, C. (1993) 'The Myth of Rising Female Employment', *Work, Employment and Society*, vol. 7, pp. 97–120

Hakim, C. (1995) 'Five Feminist Myths About Women's Employment', *British Journal of Sociology*, vol. 46, no. 3, pp. 429–455

Hardy, L. (1986a) *Exploration of the Career Histories of Selected Leading Male Nurses in England and Scotland*, Lethbridge, Canada: University of Lethbridge

Hardy, L. (1986b) 'Career Politics: the Case of Career Histories of Selected Leading Female Nurses in England and Scotland'. In R. White (ed.), *Political issues in nursing: past, present and future*, London: Wiley and Sons

Humphries, J. & Rubery, J. (eds.) (1995) *The Economics of Equal Opportunities*, London: Equal Opportunities Commission

Hutt, R. (1985) *Chief Nursing Officer Career Profiles: A Study of Backgrounds*, Brighton: Institute of Manpower Studies

IHMS Consultants (1995) *Creative Career Paths in the NHS: Report No. 4 Senior Nurses*, London: Department of Health

Joseph, G. (1983) *Women at Work: The British Experience*, Oxford: Philip Allan

Labour Research (1997) 'Women Knock on Boardroom Door', vol. 86, no. 1, pp. 125–138

Mackay, L. (1989) *Nursing a Problem*, Milton Keynes: Open University Press

Marsh, A., Ford, R. & Finlayson, L. (1997) *Lone Parents, Work and Benefits*, London: The Stationery Office

Metcalf, H. (ed) (1997) *Half Our Future: Women, Skill Development and Training*, London: Policy Studies Institute

Millward, N. & Woodland, S. (1995) 'Gender Segregation and Male/Female Wage Difference', in J. Rubery & J. Humphries (eds.) *The Economics of Equal Opportunities*, London: Equal Opportunities Commission

Mincer, J. & Polachek, S. (1974) 'Family investments in human capital: Earnings of women', *Journal of Political Economy*, vol. 82 (supplement), pp. S76–108

National Union of Public Employees (NUPE) (1992) *Women in the NHS: a Time for Positive Action*, London: NUPE

NHS Equal Opportunities Unit (1997) *Equality of Opportunity and the Health Service Workforce: Future Directions*, unpublished document

Oppenheim, A. N. (1992) *Questionnaire Design, Interviewing and Attitude Measurement*, London: Pinter Publishers Limited

Paci, P., Joshi, H. & Makepeace, G. (1995) 'Pay Gaps Facing Men and Women Born in 1958: Differences Within the Labour Market', in J. Rubery & J. Humphries (eds.) *The Economics of Equal Opportunities*, London: Equal Opportunities Commission

Plantenga, J. (1995) 'Part–Time Work and Equal Opportunities: the Case of The Netherlands', in J. Rubery & J. Humphries (eds.) *The Economics of Equal Opportunities*, London: Equal Opportunities Commission

Prechal, S. & Burrows, N. (1990) *Gender Discrimination Law of the European Community*, Aldershot: Vermont

Price Waterhouse (1988) *Nurse Retention and Recruitment*, London: Price Waterhouse

Rogers, J. (1983) *The Career Patterns of Nurses who have Completed a JBNCS Certificate: Report of the Follow–Up Study*, London: Department of Health and Social Security

Seccombe, I. & Ball, J. (1992) *Motivation, Morale and Mobility: A Profile of Qualified Nurses in the 1990s, IMS Report No. 233*, Brighton: Institute of Manpower Studies

Skevington, S. & Dawkes, D. (1988) 'Fred Nightingale', *Nursing Times*, vol. 84, no. 21,

Sloane, P.J., Murphy, P.D. & Theodossiou, I. (1993) 'Labour Market Segmentation: a Local Labour Market Analysis using Alternative Approaches', *Applied Economics*, vol. 25, pp. 569–581

Sly, F., Price, A. & Risdon, A. (1997) 'Women in the Labour Market: Results from the Spring 1996 Labour Force Survey', *Labour Market Trends*, March, pp. 91–113

Waite, R. & Hutt, R. (1987) *Attitudes, Jobs and Mobility of Qualified Nurses: A Report for the RCN, IMS Report No. 130*, Brighton: Institute of Manpower Studies

Waite, R.K., Buchan, J. & Thomas, J. (1990) *Career Patterns of Scotland's Qualified Nurses – A Report for the Scottish Home and Health Department*, Brighton: Institute of Manpower Studies

Waite, R., Buchan, J. & Thomas, J. (1989) *Nurses In and Out of Work. A Tracing Study, 1986–88 for the RCN of the Attitudes, Employment and Mobility Rates of RCN Members*, Brighton: Institute of Manpower Studies

Wajcman, J. (1996) 'The Domestic Basis for a Managerial Career', *The Sociological Review*, vol. 44, no. 4, pp. 609–629

Waldfogel, J. (1997) 'The Effect of Children on Women's Wages', *American Sociological Review*, vol. 62, pp. 209–17

Wilkinson, F. (1981) *The Dynamics of Labour Market Segmentation*, London: Academic Press

Wright, R. E. & Ermisch, J. E. (1991) 'Gender Discrimination in the British Labour Market: a Reassessment' *The Economic Journal*, vol. 101, May 1991, pp. 508–522

Confidential

Appendix 2

SURVEY ON CAREERS OF NURSING STAFF IN THE NHS

The independent POLICY STUDIES INSTITUTE is asking
your views on training, promotion, job satisfaction,
equal opportunities and changes in the NHS.

Please complete this questionnaire as soon as possible
and return it in the envelope provided. Thank you.

POLICY
STUDIES
INSTITUTE

This questionnaire is being sent to nursing staff including qualified nurses and unqualified auxiliaries and assistants. We have used the term 'nurse' throughout the questionnaire to mean all qualified nurses **including midwives and health visitors.** We have used the term 'auxiliary' throughout the questionnaire to mean all unqualified nursing staff including **nursing assistants, nursing auxiliaries, health care assistants and their equivalents.**

Please answer the questions in this questionnaire. Most of the questions can be answered by:

putting a tick in a box, like this .... ☑

or by writing in a number, like this ......*12*......

HOW YOU STARTED – EVERYONE TO ANSWER

1. **How important to you were each of the following in choosing to enter nursing or nursing auxiliary work?**

   PLEASE TICK A BOX IN EACH LINE

	Very important 4	Fairly important 3	Not very important 2	Not at all important 1	
Helping others in the community					8
A job suiting your talents					9
Opportunities for travel					10
Opportunities to take responsibility					11
Opportunities to give supervision					12
Security of employment					13
Prospects of promotion					14
Quality of initial training					15
Prospects of further training					16
Starting salary					17
Long term salary prospects					18
Flexibility of hours of work					19
Status of the job					20
Interesting work					21
Variety of work					22
Rewarding work					23
Family member or friend in nursing					24
Prospects of a career structure					25
Plenty of jobs likely to be available					26
Other reason *(please specify and tick box)*					27

   ....

1

2. What nursing qualifications have you obtained? Do not include post-basic ENB courses. (*Tick ALL that apply*)

RGN / SRN .... ☐ (28)

RMN .... ☐ (29)

RNMH .... ☐ (30)

RSCN .... ☐ (31)

EN(G), SEN .... ☐ (32)

EN(MH) .... ☐ (33)

RM, SCM .... ☐ (34)

RHV, HV cert. .... ☐ (35)

NDN cert. .... ☐ (36)

RNT .... ☐ (37)

RCNT .... ☐ (38)

NNEB .... ☐ (39)

BA / BSc Nursing .... ☐ (40)

Other (*please specify and tick box*) .... ☐ (41)

.... (41-47)

3. In what year did you first register or enrol as a qualified nurse in the UK?

Please write in year   19 ....   (48-49)

(50-54)

4. Do you have any overseas nursing qualifications?

(55)

Yes .... ☐ 1 **Go to Question 5**

No .... ☐ 2 **Go to Question 6**

5. How long did it take for you to get registered with the U.K.C.C.?

.... Years   .... Months   (56-59)

YOUR CURRENT POST – EVERYONE TO ANSWER

6. Is your current post full-time or part-time? (*Please tick ONE box and enter the number of hours for part-time*)

(60)

Full-time (35 hours or over per week) .... ☐ 1

Part-time .... ☐ 2

Job share .... ☐ 3

If part-time or job share, state hours per week .... hours   (61-62)

7. Which of these categories best describes the specialty of your current post?
(Please tick ONE box only)

(63-64)

Medical/surgical .... ☐ 1

Paediatric .... ☐ 2

Midwifery/obstetrics/gynaecology .... ☐ 3

Mental illness .... ☐ 4

Mental handicap .... ☐ 5

Care of the elderly .... ☐ 6

Health visiting .... ☐ 7

District nursing .... ☐ 8

School nursing .... ☐ 9

Practice nursing .... ☐ 10

Other *(please specify and tick box)* .... ☐ 11

....

CAREER HISTORY – EVERYONE TO ANSWER

8. Apart from any period of initial training, in which year did you get your first job as a nurse or nursing auxiliary?

Please write in year   19 ....   (65-66)

---

9. Have you had any breaks in service? By breaks we mean those periods when you were on maternity leave and periods when you were not employed by the NHS.

(67)

Yes .... ☐ 1

No .... ☐ 2 **Go to Question 13**

---

10. How many breaks in service have you had altogether?

Please write in number   ....   (68-69)

---

11. What was the length of the longest break in service?

Please write in number of years and months

.... Years .... Months   (70-73)

(74-80)

3

12. Were you doing any of the following during your breaks of service? *(Please tick ALL that apply)*

(Card 2)

Having or raising a child/ren .... ☐ (10)

Working in some other job .... ☐ (11)

Unemployed and seeking work .... ☐ (12)

Working in nursing abroad .... ☐ (13)

Working in private nursing in the UK .... ☐ (14)

In full or part-time education .... ☐ (15)

Other *(please specify and tick box)* .... ☐ (16-20)

....

13. Including your nurse training, what is the total length of your service to date (not counting any breaks)?

Please write in number of years and months

.... Years .... Months   (21-24)

14. How long have you worked in your present post, that is with your present employer and at your present grade or level (not counting any breaks)?

Please write in number of years and months

.... Years .... Months   (25-28)

(The 1988 regrading does *not* count as a new post. If your employer became a Trust, this does *not* count as a new post.)

15. Do you have any other paid work, apart from your main job?

(29)

Yes .... ☐ 1

No .... ☐ 2 **Go to Question 17**

16. What are these other jobs? *(Please tick ALL that apply)*

NHS nursing .... ☐ (30)

Bank nursing .... ☐ (31)

Agency nursing .... ☐ (32)

Non-NHS nursing .... ☐ (33)

Other job where nursing qualifications are relevant .... ☐ (34)

Job unrelated to nursing .... ☐ (35)

4

17. What is your pattern of work at present? *(Please tick ONE box only)*

(36-37)

Mix of earlies, lates and nights	☐ 1
Days only - '9 - 5' or equivalent	☐ 2
Days only - '9 - 3', school hours	☐ 3
Nights only	☐ 4
Mix of earlies and lates	☐ 5
Earlies only	☐ 6
Lates only	☐ 7
Evenings/twilight shift	☐ 8
Split shifts	☐ 9
Flexi time	☐ 10
Other *(please specify and tick box)*	☐ 11

....

18. What pattern of work would you prefer? *(Please tick ONE box only)*

(38-39)

Mix of earlies, lates and nights	☐ 1
Days only - '9 - 5' or equivalent	☐ 2
Days only - '9 - 3', school hours	☐ 3
Nights only	☐ 4
Mix of earlies and lates	☐ 5
Earlies only	☐ 6
Lates only	☐ 7
Evenings/twilight shift	☐ 8
Split shifts	☐ 9
Flexi time	☐ 10
Other *(please specify and tick box)*	☐ 11

....

19. Do you work on a duty roster?

(40)

Yes	☐ 1
No	☐ 2 **Go to Question 21**

20. When the duty rosters are being drawn up, how much influence do you have about when you will have time off? *(Please tick ONE box only)*

(41)

A great deal	☐ 4
Quite a bit	☐ 3
Not much	☐ 2
None at all	☐ 1

21. If on a particular day you wanted to swap your times of duty with another nurse/auxiliary of the same grade, would your manager or supervisor usually agree? *(Please tick ONE box only)*

(42)

Always .... ☐ 4

Usually .... ☐ 3

Sometimes .... ☐ 2

Never .... ☐ 1

Not applicable .... ☐ 0

ONLY *HEALTH VISITORS* TO ANSWER – OTHERS GO TO QUESTION 23

22. If on a particular day you wanted to swap a clinic with another health visitor of the same grade, would your manager or supervisor usually agree? *(Please tick ONE box only)*

(43)

Always .... ☐ 4

Usually .... ☐ 3

Sometimes .... ☐ 2

Never .... ☐ 1

(44-45)

EVERYONE TO ANSWER

23. Did you work any extra hours last week?

(46)

Yes .... ☐ 1

No .... ☐ 2 **Go to Question 26**

24. How many extra hours did you work last week? *(Please write in number of hours below)*

.... Hours   (47-48)

25a. Do you expect to be paid for these extra hours, or take time 'in lieu', or both, or neither?

(49)

Paid .... ☐ 3 **Answer Question 25b**

Time in lieu .... ☐ 2

Both .... ☐ 1 **Answer Question 25b**

Neither .... ☐ 0

b. How many hours do you expect to be paid for?

.... Hours   (50-51)

6

GRADING – EVERYONE TO ANSWER

26. What is your grade or equivalent (i.e. A to I)?

Please write in grade   Grade . . . .   (52)

27. Do you think that your current grade is a fair reflection of the duties and responsibilities you have at work?

(53)

Yes . . . . □ 1

No . . . . □ 2

28. Were you in NHS employment as a nurse or auxiliary at the time of the regrading in October 1988?

(54)

Yes . . . . □ 1

No . . . . □ 2   **Go to Question 32**

29. Have you appealed against your job grade since you were first informed of your new grade (October 1988)?

(55)

Yes . . . . □ 1   **Go to Question 31**

No . . . . □ 2

30. Did you ever consider appealing against your job grade?

(56)

Yes . . . . □ 1   **Go to Question 32**

No . . . . □ 2   **Go to Question 32**

31. What was the outcome of the appeal? (*Please tick ONE box only*)

(57)

Awaiting outcome . . . . □ 1

Unsuccessful . . . . □ 2

Successful . . . . □ 3

Partially successful . . . . □ 4

(58-60)

NURSING TASKS AND SATISFACTION – EVERYONE TO ANSWER

32. In your opinion how often, if at all, do you do work which should be undertaken by a lower grade of staff? (*Please tick ONE box only*)

(61)

Daily . . . . □ 4

Weekly . . . . □ 3

Monthly . . . . □ 2

Never . . . . □ 1

33. In your opinion how often, if at all, do you do work which should be undertaken by a higher grade of staff? *(Please tick ONE box only)*

(62)

Daily .... ☐ 4

Weekly .... ☐ 3

Monthly .... ☐ 2

Never .... ☐ 1

---

34. Are you a fieldwork teacher/practical workteacher of students or other staff?

(63)

Yes .... ☐ 1

No .... ☐ 2

---

35. Are you a mentor of students or other staff?

(64)

Yes .... ☐ 1

No .... ☐ 2

---

36. Are you a qualified assessor of students or other staff?

(65)

Yes .... ☐ 1

No .... ☐ 2

---

37. Are you at present 'acting up' to a higher grade post?

(66)

Yes .... ☐ 1

No .... ☐ 2

---

38. Are you at present adopting an 'extended role' in your present grade?

(67)

Yes .... ☐ 1

No .... ☐ 2

---

39. Other than anything you have already mentioned, do you have any other management responsibilities for staff?

(68)

Yes .... ☐ 1

No .... ☐ 2

(69-80)

8

40. How satisfied are you with the following in your present post?

PLEASE TICK ONE BOX IN EACH LINE	Satisfied 4	Neither satisfied nor dis-satisfied 3	Dissatisfied 2	Very dissatisfied 1	
Your basic pay					(10)
Your present workload					(11)
The amount of auxiliary support available					(12)
The amount of qualified nurse support available					(13)
The amount of administrative/clerical work you have to do					(14)
The amount of time you have for clinical nursing duties					(15)
Your security of employment					(16)
The amount of training opportunities available					(17)
Your involvement in decision making					(18)
Your promotion prospects					(19)
The opportunity to work the hours you want					(20)
Relations with colleagues					(21)
Relations with patients/clients					(22)
Overall, how satisfied are you with your present post					(23)

(24-25)

WORKING ON THE NURSE BANK

THIS SECTION IS FOR QUALIFIED AND UNQUALIFIED NURSING STAFF *WITH A PERMANENT POST WHO ALSO WORK ON THE NURSING BANK*

41. Bearing in mind that you have a permanent post, what are your reasons for also working on the nursing bank? Please indicate how important the following reasons are.

	Very important 4	Fairly important 3	Not important 2	Not at all important 1	
Earning extra money					(26)
Quicker way of gaining varied nursing experience					(27)
It is easier to fit my bank work around my studies					(28)
Unable to get a permanent post in preferred specialty					(29)
It is easier to fit my bank work around my childcare arrangements					(30)

42. How many hours have you worked on the nursing bank in the last four weeks?

Please write in number of hours .... (31-33)

9

43. Which of these categories best describes the specialty you usually work in on the nursing bank?
(Please tick ALL that apply)

Medical / surgical	☐ (34)
Paediatric	☐ (35)
Midwifery / obstetrics / gynaecology	☐ (36)
Mental illness	☐ (37)
Mental handicap	☐ (38)
Care of the elderly	☐ (39)
Health visiting	☐ (40)
District nursing	☐ (41)
School nursing	☐ (42)
Practice nursing	☐ (43)
Other *(please specify and tick box)*	☐ (44-50)

. . . .

44. What is your grade when you work for the nursing bank?

Please write in grade   . . . .   (51)

45. Do you think this grade is a fair reflection of the duties and responsiblities you have when working for the nursing bank?

(52)

Yes . . . . ☐ 1

No . . . . ☐ 2

46. Given the choice, would you prefer more paid hours in your permanent post rather than work on the nursing bank?

(53)

Yes . . . . ☐ 1

No . . . . ☐ 2

Don't know . . . . ☐ 0

47a. Do you think that black, Asian and white nurses get offered a fair share of work on the nursing bank?

(54)

Yes . . . . ☐ 1 **Qualified staff go to Question 48**
Unqualified staff to to Question 58

No . . . . ☐ 2 **Go to Question 47b**

b. If no, which group do you think is most often unfairly treated?

(55)

White nurses . . . . ☐ 1

Black or Asian nurses . . . . ☐ 2

10

TRAINING OPPORTUNITIES AND CAREER DEVELOPMENT – ONLY *QUALIFIED NURSES* TO ANSWER. AUXILIARIES AND UNQUALIFIED STAFF GO TO QUESTION 58

48a. Have you ever completed or are you currently on any post-basic clinical training courses for a recordable qualification? (i.e. those courses run by the English National Board)

DO NOT INCLUDE ENROLLED TO REGISTERED NURSE CONVERSION COURSES
(Please tick ALL that apply)

Completed course/s	☐	(56)
Currently on course/s	☐	(57)
Neither	☐	(58) **Go to Question 49**

b. How many of these post-basic recordable qualifications do you have in total?

Please write in number   . . . .   (59-60)

c. Have you ever applied to go on one of these courses?

(61)

Yes	☐	1
No	☐	2

49. On the whole, is it easy or difficult for you *to get information* on courses for nurses on your grade while you are at work? *(Please tick ONE box)*

(62)

Very easy	☐	5
Fairly easy	☐	4
Neither easy nor difficult	☐	3
Fairly difficult	☐	2
Very difficult	☐	1

50. On the whole, is it easy or difficult for you *to get paid time off* to go on courses?
(Please tick ONE box)

(63)

Very easy	☐	5
Fairly easy	☐	4
Neither easy nor difficult	☐	3
Fairly difficult	☐	2
Very difficult	☐	1

51. On the whole, is it easy or difficult for you *to get the fees of a course paid* for by your employer?
(Please tick ONE box)

(64)

Very easy	☐	5
Fairly easy	☐	4
Neither easy nor difficult	☐	3
Fairly difficult	☐	2
Very difficult	☐	1

52. On the whole, does management encourage you to go on post-basic training courses, like ENB courses for instance, or does it discourage you from going on them? *(Please tick ONE box only)*

(65)

Encourages a lot .... ☐ 5

Encourages a bit .... ☐ 4

Neither encourages or discourages .... ☐ 3

Discourages a bit .... ☐ 2

Discourages a lot .... ☐ 1

ANSWER QUESTION 53 IF YOU ARE AN *ENROLLED OR SENIOR ENROLLED NURSE;* OTHERWISE GO TO QUESTION 65

---

53. Have you ever applied for a conversion course to become a registered nurse?

(66)

Yes .... ☐ 1

No .... ☐ 2 **Go to Question 56**

---

54. Were you successful in obtaining a place on the course?

(67)

Yes .... ☐ 1

No .... ☐ 2 **Go to Question 56**

---

55. Were you seconded by your employer?

(68)

Yes .... ☐ 1 **Go to Question 65**

No .... ☐ 2 **Go to Question 65**

---

56. Do you intend to apply for a conversion course (either again or for the first time) in the next twelve months?

(69)

Yes .... ☐ 1

No .... ☐ 2

---

57. On the whole, does management encourage you to apply for a conversion course or does it discourage you from applying?

(70)

Encourages a lot .... ☐ 5

Encourages a bit .... ☐ 4

Neither encourages or discourages .... ☐ 3

Discourages a bit .... ☐ 2

Discourages a lot .... ☐ 1

ANSWER QUESTION 58 IF YOU ARE AN AUXILIARY NURSE OR UNQUALIFIED MEMBER OF STAFF; QUALIFIED NURSES GO TO QUESTION 65

58. Have you ever applied to undertake basic nurse training?

(71)

Yes .... ☐ 1

No .... ☐ 2

59a. Have you completed any work-related training courses that lead to an NVQ?

(72)

Yes .... ☐ 1 Go to Question 59b

No .... ☐ 2 Go to Question 59c

b. At what level of NVQ are you qualified?

(73)

NVQ I .... ☐ 1

NVQ II .... ☐ 2

Higher level .... ☐ 3

c. Are you currently on a work-related training course that leads to an NVQ?

(74)

Yes .... ☐ 1

No .... ☐ 2

---

60. Do you have any overseas nursing qualifications?

(75)

Yes .... ☐ 1

No .... ☐ 2

---

61. On the whole, does management encourage you *to go on further training courses* or does it discourage you from going on them? *(Please tick ONE box only)*

(76)

Encourages a lot .... ☐ 5

Encourages a bit .... ☐ 4

Neither encourages or discourages .... ☐ 3

Discourages a bit .... ☐ 2

Discourages a lot .... ☐ 1

62. On the whole, is it easy or difficult for you *to get information on courses* for auxiliaries on your grade while you are at work? *(Please tick ONE box only)*

(77)

Very easy .... □ 5

Fairly easy .... □ 4

Neither easy nor difficult .... □ 3

Fairly difficult .... □ 2

Very difficult .... □ 1

63. On the whole, is it easy or difficult for you *to get paid time off* to go on training courses? *(Please tick ONE box only)*

(78)

Very easy .... □ 5

Fairly easy .... □ 4

Neither easy nor difficult .... □ 3

Fairly difficult .... □ 2

Very difficult .... □ 1

64. On the whole, is it easy or difficult for you *to get the fees of a course paid* for by your employer? *(Please tick ONE box only)*

(79)

Very easy .... □ 5

Fairly easy .... □ 4

Neither easy nor difficult .... □ 3

Fairly difficult .... □ 2

Very difficult .... □ 1

CHILDCARE AND WORKING ARRANGEMENTS – EVERYONE TO ANSWER

65. Do you have any children under the age of 16?

(80)

Yes .... □ 1

No .... □ 2 **Go to Question 69**

66. How many of your children are under the age of 16? *(Please write in how many where appropriate)*

(Card 4)

How many of your children are aged 0-5? .... (10)

How many of your children are aged 6-16? .... (11)

14

67. Some employers give help of various kinds to parents of children up to age 16. Have you made use of any of the following with your present employer? *(Please tick ALL that apply)*

Flexible full-time working hours .... ☐ (12)

Job-sharing .... ☐ (13)

Career-break or retainer schemes .... ☐ (14)

Special shifts (e.g. evenings for parents) .... ☐ (15)

Assistance in funding child-care facilities away
from the workplace .... ☐ (16)

Financial help for the costs of child-care
(e.g. child-care vouchers) .... ☐ (17)

Facilities at the workplace for looking after young children
(e.g. creche, nursery) .... ☐ (18)

Holiday playscheme .... ☐ (19)

Other arrangements *(please specify and tick box)* .... ☐ (20-25)

....

68. In general, how good are the facilities your employer provides for parents like you with children up to the age of 16? *(Please tick ONE box only)*

(26)

Very good .... ☐ 5

Fairly good .... ☐ 4

Neither good nor bad .... ☐ 3

Fairly bad .... ☐ 2

Very bad .... ☐ 1

(27-30)

THE FUTURE – EVERYONE TO ANSWER

69. What do you expect to be doing in three years from now? *(Please tick ALL that apply)*

Nursing job in the private sector .... ☐ (31)

Better NHS nursing job (higher grade or preferred speciality) . ☐ (32)

Same nursing job and grade as present .... ☐ (33)

Same nursing job and lower grade than present .... ☐ (34)

Non-nursing job .... ☐ (35)

Full or part-time education .... ☐ (36)

Raising a family .... ☐ (37)

Nursing job overseas .... ☐ (38)

Non-nursing job overseas .... ☐ (39)

Retired .... ☐ (40)

Redundant .... ☐ (41)

Unemployed .... ☐ (42)

Other *(please specify and tick box)* .... ☐ (43-47)

....

Don't know .... ☐ (48)

GENERAL EDUCATION – EVERYONE TO ANSWER

70a. Do you have any of the qualifications listed below?

                      (49)

Yes .... ☐ ı **Answer Question 70b**

No .... ☐ 2

b. If yes, please fill in how many you have.

	How many?	
CSE or equivalent		
Grade 1	. . . .	(50-51)
Grade 2-5	. . . .	(52-53)
GCSE or equivalent		
Grade A, B or C	. . . .	(54-55)
Grade D, E, F or G	. . . .	(56-57)
GCE O level or equivalent		
Grades A, B or C, or pass before 1975	. . . .	(58-59)
Grades D or E	. . . .	(60-61)
GCE A level		
A level or Higher School Certificate or Matric	. . . .	(62)
ONC, OND, BEC, TEC, BTEC - National or General Certificate or Diploma	. . . .	(63)
HNC, HND, BEC, BTEC, TEC - Higher Certificate or Higher Diploma	. . . .	(64)
Teaching qualification	. . . .	(65)
University Diploma	. . . .	(66)
First Degree (eg. BA, BSc)	. . . .	(67)
Higher Degree (eg. MSc, PhD)	. . . .	(68)

---

71. Are you studying for a degree at present?

                      (69)

Yes .... ☐ ı

No .... ☐ 2

---

72. Apart from any ENB courses, are you studying for a diploma at present?

                      (70)

Yes .... ☐ ı

No .... ☐ 2

BACKGROUND INFORMATION – EVERYONE TO ANSWER

73. What year were you born?

Please write here   19 . . . .   (71-72)

74. Are you:

(73)

Male . . . . □ 1

Female . . . . □ 2

75. Are you: *(Please tick ONE box only)*

(74)

Married or living together . . . . □ 1

Single / widowed / divorced or separated . . . . □ 2

76. Are you currently living in: (Please tick ONE box only)

(75)

Privately owned accommodation . . . . □ 1

Privately rented accommodation . . . . □ 2

NHS accommodation . . . . □ 3

Council accommodation . . . . □ 4

Housing Association accommodation . . . . □ 5

Other *(please specify and tick box)* . . . . □ 6-9

. . . .

77. Are you a member of a trade union or professional association?

(76)

Yes . . . . □ 1

No . . . . □ 2 **Go to Question 79**

78. Which trade union or professional association do you belong to? *(Please tick ALL that apply)*

(Card 5)

UNISON (NALGO/NUPE/COHSE) . . . . □ (10)

RCN . . . . □ (11)

RCM . . . . □ (12)

HVA / MSF . . . . □ (13)

DNA . . . . □ (14)

CPNA . . . . □ (15)

Other *(please specify and tick box)* . . . . □ (16-20)

. . . .

17

79. In what country were you born?

(21-22)

United Kingdom & N. Ireland .... ☐ 1
Eire/Irish Republic .... ☐ 2

Caribbean
West Indies/Guyana .... ☐ 3

Indian Sub-Continent
India .... ☐ 4
Pakistan .... ☐ 5
Bangladesh .... ☐ 6
Sri Lanka .... ☐ 7

African Continent
Africa .... ☐ 8
Mauritius .... ☐ 9

Asia
Philippines .... ☐ 10
Hong Kong .... ☐ 11
Singapore .... ☐ 12
China .... ☐ 13
Vietnam .... ☐ 14
Malaysia .... ☐ 15

Australasia
New Zealand .... ☐ 16
Australia .... ☐ 17

Other country *(please specify and tick box)* .... ☐ 18
. . . .

**ONLY ANSWER QUESTION 80 *IF YOU WERE NOT BORN IN THE UNITED KINGDOM;*
OTHERWISE GO TO QUESTION 81**

---

80. *If you were not born in the United Kingdom,* how old were you when you moved to Britain?

Please write here . . . . Years (23-24)

18

81. Would you describe your ethnic origins as: *(Please tick ALL that apply)*

White .... ☐ (25)

Black Caribbean .... ☐ (26)

Indian Caribbean .... ☐ (27)

Black African .... ☐ (28)

Black other *(please specify and tick box)* .... ☐ (29-34)

....

Indian .... ☐ (35)

Pakistani .... ☐ (36)

Bangladeshi .... ☐ (37)

Chinese .... ☐ (38)

Other *(please specify and tick box)* .... ☐ (39-44)

....

EQUAL OPPORTUNITIES – EVERYONE TO ANSWER

82a. Do you think that applicants are ever refused nursing jobs *in the NHS* for reasons to do with their race or colour, and if so how often do you think this happens? *(Please tick ONE box only)*

(45)

No, never .... ☐ 1

Rarely .... ☐ 2 **Go to Question 82b**

Occasionally .... ☐ 3 **Go to Question 82b**

Fairly often .... ☐ 4 **Go to Question 82b**

Often .... ☐ 5 **Go to Question 82b**

b. Do you think this happens mainly to:

(46)

White nurses .... ☐ 1

Black or Asian nurses .... ☐ 2

Both .... ☐ 3

83a. Do you think that applicants are ever refused nursing jobs *in your workplace* for reasons to do with their race or colour, and if so how often do you think this happens? *(Please tick ONE box only)*

(47)

No, never .... ☐ 1

Rarely .... ☐ 2 **Go to Question 83b**

Occasionally .... ☐ 3 **Go to Question 83b**

Fairly often .... ☐ 4 **Go to Question 83b**

Often .... ☐ 5 **Go to Question 83b**

b. Do you think this happens mainly to:

(48)

White nurses .... ☐ 1

Black or Asian nurses .... ☐ 2

Both .... ☐ 3

84a. Do you think that nursing staff *in the NHS* are ever denied the opportunity to go on training courses for reasons to do with their race or colour, and if so how often do you think this happens? (*Please tick ONE box only*)

(49)

No, never .... ☐ 1

Rarely .... ☐ 2 **Go to Question 84b**

Occasionally .... ☐ 3 **Go to Question 84b**

Fairly often .... ☐ 4 **Go to Question 84b**

Often .... ☐ 5 **Go to Question 84b**

b. Do you think this happens mainly to:

(50)

White nurses .... ☐ 1

Black or Asian nurses .... ☐ 2

Both .... ☐ 3

85a. Do you think that nursing staff in your workplace are ever denied the opportunity to go on training courses for reasons to do with their race or colour, and if so how often do you think this happens? (*Please tick ONE box only*)

(51)

No, never .... ☐ 1

Rarely .... ☐ 2 **Go to Question 85b**

Occasionally .... ☐ 3 **Go to Question 85b**

Fairly often .... ☐ 4 **Go to Question 85b**

Often .... ☐ 5 **Go to Question 85b**

b. Do you think this happens mainly to:

(52)

White nurses .... ☐ 1

Black or Asian nurses .... ☐ 2

Both .... ☐ 3

---

86. While working in the NHS, have you yourself ever been refused a job for reasons to do with your race or colour, and if so when did this last happen? (*Please tick ONE box only*)

(53)

No, never .... ☐ 1

Within the past year .... ☐ 2

Within the past five years .... ☐ 3

Over five years ago .... ☐ 4

---

87. While working in the NHS, have you yourself ever been refused a promotion for reasons to do with your race or colour, and if so when did this last happen? (*Please tick ONE box only*)

(54)

No, never .... ☐ 1

Within the past year .... ☐ 2

Within the past five years .... ☐ 3

Over five years ago .... ☐ 4

88. While working in the NHS, have you yourself ever been refused a training opportunity for reasons to do with your race or colour, and if so when did this last happen? *(Please tick ONE box only)*

(55)

No, never .... ☐ 1

Within the past year .... ☐ 2

Within the past five years .... ☐ 3

Over five years ago .... ☐ 4

89. Do patients or their families ever behave towards you in a difficult, aggressive or hostile way for reasons to do with your race or colour, and if so how often does this happen? *(Please tick ONE box only)*

(56)

No, never .... ☐ 1

Daily .... ☐ 2

Weekly .... ☐ 3

Monthly .... ☐ 4

Less often .... ☐ 5

90. Do members of the nursing staff (including supervisors or managers) ever behave towards you in a difficult, aggressive or hostile way for reasons to do with your race or colour, and if so how often does this happen? *(Please tick ONE box only)*

(57)

No, never .... ☐ 1

Daily .... ☐ 2

Weekly .... ☐ 3

Monthly .... ☐ 4

Less often .... ☐ 5

91. Does your employer have a policy of ensuring equal opportunities for people from all racial or ethnic groups? *(Please tick ONE box only)*

(58)

Yes .... ☐ 1

No .... ☐ 2 **Go to Question 93**

Don't know .... ☐ 3 **Go to Question 93**

92. How effective do you think it is? *(Please tick ONE box only)*

(59)

Very effective .... ☐ 4

Fairly effective .... ☐ 3

Not very effective .... ☐ 2

Not effective at all .... ☐ 1

93. *In the regrading of 1988,* do you think that white and ethnic minority nursing staff were treated equally, or that one or other group was given much better or somewhat better treatment? *(Please tick ONE box only)*

(60)

White and ethnic minority nursing staff given equal treatment ☐ 1

Ethnic minority staff given much better treatment .... ☐ 2

Ethnic minority staff given somewhat better treatment ...... ☐ 3

White staff given much better treatment .... ☐ 4

White staff given somewhat better treatment .... ☐ 5

Don't know .... ☐ 6

94. On the whole, do you think that ethnic minorities and white people have *equal chances in nursing in the NHS,* or that one or other group has much better or somewhat better chances? *(Please tick ONE box only)*

(61)

White and ethnic minority people have equal chances .... ☐ 1

Ethnic minorities have much better chances .... ☐ 2

Ethnic minorities have somewhat better chances .... ☐ 3

White people have much better chances .... ☐ 4

White people have somewhat better chances .... ☐ 5

Don't know .... ☐ 6

95. Finally, please use the space below for any other comments you would like to make about any of the questions we have asked you.

....

....

....

....

....

We would like to contact you again in a year's time to find out how your career has progressed and whether you are still in nursing. To enable us to contact you, would you please write your name, home address and telephone number below.

....

....

....

This information will be used only to contact you again in connection with this study.

Thank you very much for your help. Now please post the questionnaire in the enclosed stamped addressed envelope. All your answers will be treated IN COMPLETE CONFIDENCE.